How to Beat Your Competitors

AF663913

Published by :
Lotus Press Publishers & Distributors

How to Beat Your Competitors

S.C. Gupta

Lotus PRESS
4735/22, Prakash Deep Building
Ansari Road, Darya Ganj,
New Delhi - 110002

Lotus Press : Publishers & Distributors
Unit No. 220, 2nd Floor, 4735/22, Prakash Deep Building,
Ansari Road, Darya Ganj, New Delhi- 110002
Ph.: 23280047, 98118-38000
• E-mail : lotuspress1984@gmail.com
www.lotuspress.co.in

How to Beat Your Competitors
© **2025, S.C. Gupta**
ISBN: 978-81-8382-217-6

All rights reserved. No part of this publication may be reproduced, stored in a retrieval system, or transmitted, in any form or by any means, mechanical, photocopying, recording or otherwise, without prior written permission of the publishers.

Printed & Published by : **Lotus Press Publishers & Distributors,** New Delhi-02

Preface

Are you a CEO, manager, or entrepreneur? A consultant, author, or speaker? Or a doctor, lawyer, idea person, or inventor? Whoever you are, and whatever you do, you have a unique factor--that special element only you can deliver to your business that will satisfy and delight your customers and clients. And whether you already have a dream career whose potential you want to maximize, or are just starting to make your way in your profession, you need to target that seed of success that will put you on the map and make you a household name.

This book presents guidelines on how to beat your business competitors and explains how to develop a competitor intelligence programme without a large investment in business or staff, why the low-tech" route is often the most effective, how to communicate intelligence information to the decision makers. This book explains how to develop business strategies to outcome and overwhelm your business competitors from the market.

- Author

Contents

1
Competitor Analysis

Competitor analysis in marketing and strategic management is an assessment of the strengths and weaknesses of current and potential competitors. This analysis provides both an offensive and defensive strategic context through which to identify opportunities and threats. Competitor profiling coalesces all of the relevant sources of competitor analysis into one framework in the support of efficient and effective strategy formulation, implementation, monitoring and adjustment.

Given that competitor analysis is an essential component of corporate strategy, it is argued that most firms do not conduct this type of analysis systematically enough. Instead, many enterprises operate on what is called "informal impressions, conjectures, and intuition gained through the tidbits of information about competitors every manager continually receives." As a result, traditional environmental scanning places many firms at risk of dangerous competitive blind spots due to a lack of robust competitor analysis.

Marketing should include competitor analysis. Who are your competitors? What customer needs and preferences are you competing to meet? What are the similarities and differences between their products/services and yours? What are the strengths and weaknesses of each of their products and services? How do their prices compare to yours? How are they doing overall? How do you plan to complete? Offer better quality services? Lower prices? More support? Easier access to services? How are you uniquely suited to compete with them?

Why Bother to Analyse Competitors?

Some businesses think it is best to get on with their own plans and ignore the competition. Others become obsessed with tracking the actions of competitors (often using underhand or illegal methods). Many businesses are happy simply to track the competition, copying their moves and reacting to changes.

Competitor analysis has several important roles in strategic planning:

- to help management understand their competitive advantages/disadvantages relative to competitors
- to generate understanding of competitors' past, present (and most importantly) future strategies
- to provide an informed basis to develop strategies to achieve competitive advantage in the future
- to help forecast the returns that may be made from future investments (e.g. how will competitors respond to a new product or pricing strategy?)

Competitor Array

One common and useful technique is constructing a competitor array. The steps include:

- Define your industry - scope and nature of the industry
- Determine who your competitors are
- Determine who your customers are and what benefits they expect

Similarly, defensive strategy can be employed more deftly in order to counter the threat of rival firms from exploiting the firm's own weaknesses.

Clearly, those firms practicing systematic and advanced competitor profiling have a significant advantage. As such, a comprehensive profiling capability is rapidly becoming a core competence required for successful competition. An appropriate analogy is to consider this advantage as akin to having a good idea of the next move that your opponent in a chess match will make. By staying one move ahead, checkmate is one step closer. Indeed, as in chess, a good offense is the best defense in the game of business as well.

A common technique is to create detailed profiles on each of your major competitors. These profiles give an in-depth description of the competitor's background, finances, products, markets, facilities, personnel, and strategies. This involves.

Background

- location of offices, plants, and online presences.
- history - key personalities, dates, events and trends.
- ownership, corporate governance and organisational structure.

Financials

- P-E ratios, dividend policy, and profitability of various financial ratios, liquidity, and cash flow.
- profit growth profile; method of growth (organic or acquisitive).

Products

- Products offered, depth and breadth of product line, and product portfolio balance.

- Determine what the key success factors are in your industry.
- Rank the key success factors by giving each one a weighting - The sum of all the weightings must add up to ones.
- Rate each competitor on each of the key success factors.
- Multiply each cell in the matrix by the factor weighting.
- Sum columns for a weighted assessment of the overall strength of each competitor relative to each other.

This can best be displayed on a two dimensional matrix-competitors along the top and key success factors down the side.

Competitor Profiling

The strategic rationale of competitor profiling is powerfully simple. Superior knowledge of rivals offers a legitimate source of competitive advantage. The raw material of competitive advantage consists of offering superior customer value in the firm's chosen market. The definitive characteristic of customer value is the adjective, superior. Customer value is defined relative to rival offerings making competitor knowledge an intrinsic component of corporate strategy. Profiling facilitates this strategic objective in three important ways. First, profiling can reveal strategic weaknesses in rivals that the firm may exploit. Second, the proactive stance of competitor profiling will allow the firm to anticipate the strategic response of their rivals to the firm's planned strategies, the strategies of other competing firms, and changes in the environment. Third, this proactive knowledge will give the firms strategic agility. Offensive strategy can be implemented more quickly in order to exploit opportunities and capitalize on strengths.

- new products developed, new product success rate, and R&D strengths.
- brands, strength of brand portfolio, brand loyalty and brand awareness.
- patents and licenses.
- quality control conformance.
- reverse engineering.

Marketing

- segments served, market shares, customer base, growth rate, and customer loyalty.
- promotional mix, promotional budgets, advertising themes, ad agency used, sales force success rate, online promotional strategy.
- distribution channels used (direct & indirect), exclusivity agreements, alliances, and geographical coverage.
- pricing, discounts, and allowances.

Facilities

- plant capacity, capacity utilisation rate, age of plant, plant efficiency, capital investment.
- location, shipping logistics, and product mix by plant.

Personnel

- number of employees, key employees, and skill sets.
- strength of management, and management style.
- compensation, benefits, and employee morale & retention rates.

Corporate and Marketing Strategies

- objectives, mission statement, growth plans, acquisitions, and divestitures.
- marketing strategies.

Media Scanning

Scanning competitor's ads can reveal much about what that competitor believes about marketing and their target market. Changes in a competitor's advertising message can reveal new product offerings, new production processes, a new branding strategy, a new positioning strategy, a new segmentation strategy, line extensions and contractions, problems with previous positions, insights from recent marketing or product research, a new strategic direction, a new source of sustainable competitive advantage, or value migrations within the industry. It might also indicate a new pricing strategy such as penetration, price discrimination, price skimming, product bundling, joint product pricing, discounts, or loss leaders. It may also indicate a new promotion strategy such as push, pull, balanced, short term sales generation, long term image creation, informational, comparative, affective, reminder, new creative objectives, new unique selling proposition, new creative concepts, appeals, tone, and themes, or a new advertising agency. It might also indicate a new distribution strategy, new distribution partners, more extensive distribution, more intensive distribution, a change in geographical focus, or exclusive distribution. Little of this intelligence is definitive: additional information is needed before conclusions should be drawn.

A competitor's media strategy reveals budget allocation, segmentation and targeting strategy, and selectivity and focus. From a tactical perspective, it can also be used to help a manager implement his own media plan. By knowing the competitor's media buy, media selection, frequency, reach, continuity, schedules, and flights, the manager can arrange his own media plan so that they do not coincide.

Other sources of corporate intelligence include trade shows, patent filings, mutual customers, annual reports, and trade associations.

Some firms hire competitor intelligence professionals to obtain this information. The Society of Competitive Intelligence Professionals maintains a listing of individuals who provide these services.

New Competitors

In addition to analyzing current competitors, it is necessary to estimate future competitive threats. The most common sources of new competitors are:

- companies competing in a related product/market.
- companies using related technologies.
- companies already targeting your prime market segment but with unrelated products.
- companies from other geographical areas and with similar products.
- new start-up companies organised by former employees and/or managers of existing companies.

The entrance of new competitors is likely when:

- there are high profit margins in the industry.
- there is unmet demand (insufficient supply) in the industry.
- there are no major barriers to entry.
- there is future growth potential.
- competitive rivalry is not intense.
- gaining a competitive advantage over existing firms is feasible.

Sources of Information for Competitor Analysis

The sources of competitor information can be neatly grouped into three categories:

- Recorded data: this is easily available in published form either internally or externally. Good examples include competitor annual reports and product brochures;
- Observable data: this has to be actively sought and often assembled from several sources. A good example is competitor pricing;
- Opportunistic data: to get hold of this kind of data requires a lot of planning and organisation. Much of it is "anecdotal", coming from discussions with suppliers, customers and, perhaps, previous management of competitors.

The table below lists possible sources of competitor data:

Recorded Data	Observable Data	Opportunistic Data
Annual report & accounts	Pricing / price lists	Meetings with suppliers
Press releases	Advertising campaigns	Trade shows
Newspaper articles	Promotions	Sales force meetings
Analysts reports	Tenders	Seminars/ conferences
Regulatory reports	Patent applications	Recruiting ex-employees
Government reports		Discussion with shared distributors
Presentations / speeches		Social contacts with competitors

Each individual piece of data does not have much value. The important skill is to collect as many of the pieces as possible and to assemble them into an overall picture of the competitor. This enables you to identify any missing pieces and to take the necessary steps to collect them.

Need to know about their Competitors

Read the points below to learn about the competitor information that would help businesses complete some good quality competitor analysis.

You can probably think of many more pieces of information about a competitor that would be useful. However, an important challenge in competitor analysis is working out how to obtain competitor information that is reliable, up-to-date and available legally.

What businesses probably already know their competitors?

- Overall sales and profits.
- Sales and profits by market.
- Sales by main brand.
- Cost structure.
- Market shares (revenues and volumes).
- Organisation structure.
- Distribution system.
- Identity / profile of senior management.
- Advertising strategy and spending.
- Customer / consumer profile & attitudes.
- Customer retention levels.

What businesses would really like to know about competitors?

- Sales and profits by product.
- Relative cost.
- Customer satisfaction and service levels.
- Customer retention levels.
- Distribution costs.

- New product strategies.
- Size and quality of customer databases.
- Advertising effectiveness.
- Future investment strategy.
- Contractual terms with key suppliers.
- Terms of strategic partnerships.

The Customers' Perspective

When you start thinking about competitive analysis, ask yourself this question: What do your customers see when they compare you to your competition?

This topic covers competitive analysis from your customers' perspective. After all, your customers' perspective is the only one that counts. Knowing and understanding what the customer sees is the most important competitive analysis.

One part of being a professional advertiser is thinking like the prospective customer. Your customers and prospects do not live in a vacuum. They are sophisticated shoppers. Their perceptions of price, value, quality, and service are very high. What happens when they compare you to the competition?

Sometimes you can focus so much on what is special about your own company that you forget about your competition. But your customers and prospects will see and read your competitors' marketing materials. They are going to talk to them on the phone. They are going to price their products, review their guarantees, and meet with their sales people. Your customers will conduct their own competitive analysis.

You must do the same thing. It is very important for you to make these same contacts with your competitors so that you can understand what the customer sees. You need to know where you stand in comparison to your competitors from the customer's perspective. Conduct your competitive analysis the way your customer would.

You don't conduct a competitive analysis to copy the competition. You could be copying systems or methods that do not really work that well. This is about understanding what your customers and prospects see, think, and understand.

And don't worry if you can't afford to sell the same way a large corporation can, because you probably don't want to anyway. It is how you differentiate yourself from your competitor that counts. Your competitive analysis should determine how you are different and special, not how you are the same.

What differentiates you from your competitors from the customer's perspective? What strengths and weaknesses do you have? What strengths and weaknesses do your competitors have? What is your potential customer seeing and thinking? The answers are probably found in the difference between your advertising and marketing materials, and your competitors'.

The answers are at your fingertips. The best competitive analysis you can do is to compare your brochure to your competitors. How good is the copywriting? How professional is the presentation? You must run a competitive analysis on all of your competitors' marketing.

Without knowing the answers, you can never take advantage of your strengths, or compensate for your weaknesses from your customers' perspective. Because you can be absolutely sure of one thing - your customers will conduct their own competitive analysis.

Do you really want to beat your competitors - like-a-drum? Make sure that what your potential customers see about you is better than what they see about your competitors. Plan your marketing materials and presentations to take advantage of your strengths and of your competition's weaknesses.

Plan what your potential customers see when they compare you to your competition. Get the insight into your customer's wants, needs, and desires, and market your company to address their concerns better than your competition does. Make sure your competitive analysis is done from the customers' perspective.

Make sure you get the Customer Perspective

Businesses that fail, often forget to seek out the customer perspective. I have talked to some folks at businesses that were less than successful, and when asked if they actively seek out customer comments, the answer invariably is no. Why don't they do that? Why not get the customer perspective?

Oftentimes, the company is overconfident, and thinks they know what customers want. This myth, because that's what it is, can be upheld as long as the customer is not involved. However, the customer has a strong vote in the buying process, and in the end it will become crystal clear how the customer feels! At that point, of course, it's too late to do anything about it.

Another reason for not asking the customer is fear. From the customer perspective you might not be doing as well as you thought you were. For insecure persons that may come as a blow! In order to protect themselves, some folks just don't want to hear it and simply don't ask. On the other hand, they could be missing out on a whole lot of uplifting comments.

Get real! Would you rather get the customer's votes in your wallet, or in your mailbox?

The sooner you know how the customer feels about your business, the sooner you can start to correct any shortcomings that may emerge. But you have to act. There is no use in hiding the remarks you don't like. This doesn't change the reality. Put your customer in the centre of your business and let the rest follow in tune.

This can only improve your bottom.

Effective Competitive Analysis

For your small business to succeed, you need to know almost as much about your competitors as you do about your own company and customers. Unfortunately, many small business owners make the mistake of waiting until a competitor has opened up shop across the street and is cutting into profits to find out who and what they're up against.

A competitive analysis allows you to identify your competitors and evaluate their respective strengths and weaknesses. By knowing the actions of your competitors, you will have a better understanding of what products or services you should offer; how you can market them effectively; and how you can position your business.

Competitive analysis is an ongoing process. You should always be gathering information about your competitors. Look at their Websites. Read their product literature and brochures. Get your hands on their products. See how they present themselves at trade shows. Read about them in your industry's trade publications. Talk to your customers to see how they feel about competitive products or services.

Read the steps to learn more about how to analyse your competitors:

- **Step 1: Identify your Competition**

  Every business has competitors, and you need to take the time to discern who your customers can approach to get a product or service that fills the same need as yours does. Even if your product or service is truly innovative, you need to look at what else your customers would purchase to accomplish this task. For example, you may be opening a Website that offers online Bingo. Your competition would be other Bingo sites, other Web gaming sites, the Bingo hail down the street, and any other businesses that are competing for the same leisure-time dollars.

  Begin by looking at your primary competitors. These are the market leaders, the companies who currently dominate your market. They are probably the ones who you find yourself bumping up against in your search for new customers. If you're a florist, it would be other florists in your neighbourhood. If you're a computer consultant, it would be other consultants with the same speciality.

  Next, look for your secondary and indirect competitors. These are the businesses who may not go head-to-head with you, but who are targeting the same general market. Sticking with the florist example, it might be a small local roses-only store, a national floral delivery service, or the flower/plant department of your local supermarket or discount store.

  Finally, look at potential competitors. These are companies who might be moving into your market and who you need to prepare to compete against. For, example, you might have an independent frozen yoghurt stand; you will need to prepare to compete against national frozen yoghurt franchises, even if they are not yet in your market.

- **Step 2: Analyze Strengths and Weaknesses**

  After you've figured out who your competitors are, determine their strengths and find out what their vulnerabilities are. Why do customers buy from them. Is it price? value? service? convenience? reputation? Focus as much on "perceived" strengths and weaknesses as you do on actual ones. This is because customer perception may actually be more important than reality.

  It's a good idea to do this strengths/weaknesses analysis in table form. Write down the names of each of your competitors. Then set up columns listing every important category for your line of business (price, value, service, location, reputation, expertise, convenience, personnel, advertising/marketing, or whatever else is appropriate to your type of company). Once you have this table set, rate your competitors, and be sure to put in comments as to why you've given them that rating. You might even want to put strengths in red and weaknesses in blue, so you can tell at a glance where each competitor stands.

- **Step 3: Look at Opportunities and Threats**

  Strengths and weaknesses are often factors that are under a company's control. But when you're looking at your competition, you also need to examine how well prepared they are to deal with factors outside their control. These are called opportunities and threats.

  Opportunities and threats fall into a wide range of categories. It might be technological developments, regulatory or legal action, economic factors, or even a possible new competitor. For example, a photo developing store needs to know how well its competitors are prepared to deal with the advent of digital photography. Or a company that sells over the Web should analyse how its competitors are prepared to deal with online security issues.

Again, an effective way to do this is to create a table listing your competitors and the outside factors that will impact your industry. You will then be able to tell how they can deal with opportunities and threats.

- **Step 4: Determine your Position**

  Once you figure out what your competitors' strengths and weaknesses are, you need to determine where to position your company vis a vis the competition. Some of this may be obvious from the results of your analysis, but it also pays to take a hard look at how your business operates.

  One of the most effective ways to do this is to create a strengths/weaknesses opportunities! threats analysis of your business. Rank your company in the same categories that you ranked your competitors. This will give you an even clearer picture of where your business fits in the competitive environment. It will also help you determine what areas you need to improve, and what characteristics of your business you should take advantage of to gain more customers.

Tips for Doing Competitive Analysis

For anyone trying to grow a business, one of the first tasks is to map the competitive landscape. With a good understanding of the competition facing your company, you'll be able to spot and exploit opportunities as they develop. These dozen points should help you draw and refine your map, beginning with your earliest efforts to plan your new venture and continuing for as long as you stay in business.

1. **Be a customer**

    Bring a notepad and pencil to competing establishments and ask a lot of questions. Testing a firm's ability to serve you will reveal much about their business. And don't just pretend to shop from competitors. Buy something. It's the only way to gain first-hand experience with the company's products and services.

2. **Find out as much as you can about the people who run competing businesses**

    Where did they go to school? Where have they worked? How long have they been in the business? What are their strengths and weaknesses? This information can help you anticipate your competition's moves. For example, a local, life-long farmer will run an Indiana seed company very differently than will a young MBA.

3. **Buy stock in your competitors**

    If you're competing against a publicly traded firm, consider buying a few shares of its stock. That way you'll receive regular updates on the firm's financial results and business strategies.

4. **Talk to your competitors customers**

    Why do they buy from your competitors? Is it because of the quality of the product or service, the price, the location, or the customer support? What do they dislike about the company? What do they wish that company would provide? Why don't they buy from you?

5. **Use the internet**

    Online services such as Dow Jones Interactive allow you to search through thousands of publications for information about your competitors, especially if they include large companies. Searches are free, but you'll have to pay a fee for articles on Dow Jones or for a monthly subscription. You also can learn a great deal about competing businesses simply by going to their Websites.

6. **Check public filings**

   As an entrepreneur, you already know that companies must disclose information to government agencies. Such disclosures are required to undertake public offerings, receive building permits, register for patents or trademarks and soon. Many of those filings are public record and contain information about the company's goals, strategies, and technologies.

7. **Get to know librarians**

   Many are virtuoso researchers and can save you a great deal of time and effort. Your library also will have local publications that may have information on competitors in your areas.

8. **Attend industry conferences and trade shows**

   Your competitors' representatives will be pounding their chests about their firms' products or services. Take advantage of the opportunity to familiarise yourself with their product offerings and strategies, and how they sell themselves.

9. **Assess the competition's goals**

   A competitor trying to increase its market share might lower prices; a firm attempting to increase profits may cut costs; and a business that wants to accelerate sales growth might kick off a marketing campaign. If you know your competitors' goals, you'll be better able to anticipate their strategies..!

10. **Be aware of the potential for new Competitor**

    These days, the competitive landscape can change faster than Net-stock valuations. A national chain may not have entered your region yet-but what if it does? Likewise, companies that don't currently compete with yours might shift their focus and pit themselves against your firm.

11. **Don't delegate the job of keeping up with competitors**

    You might appoint someone to work with you on the task, doing research and the like. But as the entrepreneur, you're in the best position to appreciate and act upon information about your competitors.

12. **Define the competitive landscape broadly**

    Your competition includes anything that could draw customers away from your business. For example, movie theatres compete not only with other cinemas, but also with restaurants, live music venues, theatre - 1 even cable TV, video rentals, and video games.

Competitive Analysis - Easy Examples

If your competitors are bad at answering the phone, and you use a great employee to answer your phones, you win. If people are calling from your yellow page ad, or anyplace else for that matter, then the single most important thing you can do is improve the quality of your phone skills. Your competitive analysis will tell you how good your competitors' are. First impressions count.

McDonalds won over millions of customers by providing cleaner restrooms. But you never thought about that. What do the customers see? What's important to them? What are the impressions you make versus your competitors? Your competitive analysis will tell you.

Take a good look at your brochure versus your competitors'. Is it twice as good? What company would the customer choose if your brochure was twice as good as your competitors'?

More than this, do your competitors even have brochures, or something to send or leave with potential clients? Don't think a cheap flyer will do the trick, but if you are the only company distributing brochures, or refrigerator magnets, or coupons, or information booklets, then you will win the business. People need to think, reference, and read before they decide. Give them what they need. Your competitive analysis will show you the way.

And just how slick are all of your marketing materials? How good is your presentation? First impressions count. It is natural to be impressed by a high quality presentation and superior marketing materials. You must conduct a competitive analysis on your own company. Remember, customers are conducting their own competitive analysis - How do you compare?

❑❑❑

2
Organisational Infrastructure

For many of us, the thrill of leadership comes from inventing products, seizing opportunities and anticipating consumer needs. Yet, building infrastructure is like going to the doctor: you can survive without it, but you'll be better for it.

Infrastructure can be defined as the basic physical and organisational structures needed for the operation of a society or enterprise, or the services and facilities necessary for an economy to function. The term typically refers to the technical structures that support a society, such as roads, water supply, sewers, power grids, telecommunications, and so forth. Viewed functionally, infrastructure facilitates the production of goods and services; for example, roads enable the transport of raw materials to a factory, and also for the distribution of finished products to markets. In some contexts, the term may also include basic social services such as schools and hospitals. In military parlance, the term refers to the buildings and permanent installations necessary for the support, redeployment, and operation of military forces.

Organisational infrastructure will be used in the sense of technical structures or physical networks that support society, unless specified otherwise.

Types of Infrastructure

The following list is limited to capital assets that serve the function of conveyance or channelling of people, vehicles, fluids, energy or information, and which take the form either of a network or of a critical node used by vehicles, or used for the transmission of electro-magnetic waves. Infrastructure systems include both the fixed assets and the control systems and software required to operate, manage and monitor the systems, as well as any accessory buildings, plants or vehicles that are an essential part of the system.

Transportation Infrastructure

- Road and highway networks, including structures (bridges, tunnels, culverts, retaining walls), signage and markings, electrical systems (street lighting and traffic lights) and edge treatments (curbs, sidewalks, landscaping).
- Railways, including structures, terminal facilities (railyards, train stations), level crossings, signalling and communications systems.
- Canals and navigable waterways requiring continuous maintenance (dredging, etc.).
- Seaports and lighthouses.
- Airports, including air navigational systems.
- Mass transit systems (Commuter rail systems, subways, tramways, trolleys and bus terminals).
- Bicycle paths and pedestrian walkways.

Energy Infrastructure

- Electrical power network, including generation plants, electric grid, substations and local distribution.
- Natural gas pipelines, storage and distribution terminals, as well as the local distribution network.
- Petroleum pipelines, including associated storage and distribution terminals.

- Steam or hot water production and distribution networks for district heating systems.

Water Management Infrastructure

- Drinking water supply, including the system of pipes, pumps, valves, filtration and treatment equipment and meters, including buildings and structures to house the equipment, used for the collection, treatment and distribution of drinking water.
- Sewage collection and disposal.
- Drainage systems (storm sewers, ditches, etc).
- Major irrigation systems (reservoirs, irrigation canals)
- Major flood control systems (dikes, levees, major pumping stations and floodgates).

Communications Infrastructure

- Telephone networks (land lines) including switching systems.
- Mobile phone networks.
- Cable television networks including receiving stations and cable distribution networks.
- Internet backbone, including high-speed data cables, routers and servers as well as the protocols and other basic software required for the system to function.
- Communication satellites.
- Undersea cables.
- Major private, government or dedicated telecommunications networks, such as those used for internal communication and monitoring by major infrastructure companies, by governments, by the military or by emergency services.
- Pneumatic tube mail distribution networks.

Waste Management Facilities

- Solid waste landfills
- Solid waste incinerators
- Hazardous waste disposal facilities

Geophysical Monitoring Networks

- Meteorological monitoring networks
- Tidal and fluviometric monitoring networks
- Seismometer networks
- Remote sensing satellites

Other Systems or Networks

- Global Positioning System

Note: Certain systems or facilities that are similar to infrastructure are not included in this list because they are essentially services performed by people (commuter bus services, garbage collection services, emergency services) or they are facilities that are not necessarily part of or in the form of a network (parks, sports facilities), or they are essentially privately-owned industrial plants that do not necessarily depend on a fixed distribution network (oil refineries). However solid waste disposal facilities were included because they are often the critical nodal points of a network-like public service (garbage collection), and are usually publicly owned or heavily regulated. Telecommunication systems are included if their function is limited to the conveyance of information (telephone system), but not if their function includes supplying the content of that information (TV or radio networks).

Importance of Infrastructure

Infrastructure is especially important for young organisation looking to move to the next level. Young organisations typically overflow with passion and innovation. The organisation probably started with a passionate vision, like the idea of a simple navigation tool for an increasingly complex Internet that catapulted Yahoo to success. Early innovators may have developed products in a garage, as did Apple Computer Inc. founders Steve Jobs and Steve Wozniak with the first Apple computer. These patterns were necessary for growing the organisation.

But now, as the company matures, are youthful patterns encouraging inconsistent customer service? May be tasks are falling through the cracks because it's not clear who is responsible for what. Or perhaps people waste time reinventing the product development process for each customer.

Organisation infrastructure links goals, activities and people through planned processes and systems. Most likely, you have infrastructure to support your finances because the IRS insists upon it. What many young companies lack is infrastructure to support process and performance?

To build process infrastructure, start with the obvious: What product or service do you provide to the customer? Then back up to the very beginning: what materials, data, ideas, or supplies do you use to create that product or service?

The next step is where it can get complicated, but is also where organisations find value. Bring together representatives from each stage of the development process to map the steps that take the product from raw material to customer. If they resist (as they might, since young organisations enjoy their flexibility and often reject attempts to standardise), take the steps up one level.

Defining high-level activities provides people with a common understanding of how work gets done. Better yet, the organisation gains efficiency and consistency that customers appreciate.

After identifying and validating internal processes, you can build performance infrastructure to support employee achievement. You probably have high-level annual goals for your organisation. But how well do those high-level goals connect to your processes and people?

Seagate Technology, a pioneer in hard drive development, built a best-in-class system that links the entire organisation around a common set of goals. Seagate's senior executives come together to review goals and make sure that initiatives are aligned. Then, the executives cascade the goals through the organisation to individual levels.

Your organisation doesn't need to have sales of $7 billion like Seagate to benefit from this kind of system. Begin by bringing together your top leadership to set high-level goals. Then connect those goals to your process.

Finally, cascade the goals to every employee so that everyone understands how they help contribute to the big picture. By doing so, you'll trace a clear line from each individual to corporate goals and assure that you're well positioned to achieve every strategy.

The last step is to monitor and manage goals throughout the year. Some companies set goals in January and then forget about them until December. Don't let this happen in your company. Information about goals is a powerful motivator for performance and change. Just sharing this information can help keep the organisation aligned and focused. Every large company begins small, and every one needs infrastructure. If you want your company to shift out of survival mode and take the next step toward becoming a Yahoo, Apple, or Seagate, build the organisational infrastructure to support your growth.

Finally understanding the symptoms and diagnosing the conditions that may point to infrastructure problems-in the context of what matters most: your organisations mission, vision, values, critical success factors, and required results. By focusing on how your organisation is designed, how well all who are involved in your success understand and work collaboratively to accomplish the organisation's goals, and by creating an optimal, aligned human and organisation-system, your infrastructure will be a source of competitive advantage rather than an obstacle to getting the outcomes and results that you need.

❑❑❑

3
Business Networking

Introduction

Business networking is a marketing method by which business opportunities are created through networks of like-minded business people. There are several prominent business networking organisations that create models of networking activity that, when followed, allow the business person to build new business relationship and generate business opportunities at the same time.

Many business people contend business networking is a more cost-effective method of generating new business than advertising or public relations efforts. This is because business networking is a low-cost activity that involves more personal commitment than company money.

As an example, a business network may agree to meet weekly or monthly with the purpose of exchanging business leads and referrals with fellow members. To complement this activity, members often meet outside this circle, on their own time, and build their own "one-to-one" relationship with the fellow member.

Business networking can be conducted in a local business community, or on a more larger scale via the Internet. Business networking websites have grown over recent years due to the internets ability to connect people from all over the world.

Business networking can have a meaning also in the ICT domain, i.e. the provision of operating support to companies / organisations, and related value chains / value networks.

It refers to an activity coordination with a wider scope and a simpler implementation than pre-organized work flows or web-based impromptu searches for transaction counterparts (workflow is useful to coordinate activities, but it is complicated by the use of s.c. "patterns" to deviate the flow of work from a pure sequence, in order to compensate its intrinsic "linearity"; impromptu searches for transaction counterparts on the web are useful as well, but only for non-strategic supplies; both are complicated by a plethora of interfaces -- SOA / XML / web services -- needed among different organisations and even between different IT applications within the same organisation).

Tackling Competition

Several organisations implement Information Technology to improvise the business. This introduces competition in the world of information technology. The major factors determining the competition in the market are bargaining power of suppliers, buyers bargaining power, new entrants, effect of substitute products or services, intensity of the competition, standing in the conventional business rivals and many more. It is also important to understand the possibility of re-engineering the core business value and modify the basis of the competition. The business relationship and power among the buyers and suppliers needs to be balanced.

The organisation needs to find out ways to reduce the barriers in the entry for the customers because of the competition. It is also important to understand the importance of increasing or decreasing the switching cost. The possibility of adding values and services to the existing products to create new product lines using information technology needs to be tried out. Poor understanding of the base of the dynamics in the market within which the organisation competes can lead to big failure while implementing IT in business.

There is a need to understand the long term impact of strategic system launched by a counterpart or another industry in the competitive market. Launch a system which can bring out litigation and regulate the detriment of the innovator. The other factors to be considered for understanding the challenges in managing the competition in the IT business network are failure to account for the time, effort and expenditure required to ensure user adoption, understanding and effective utilisation.

Managing Intellectual Property Rights

It is understood that the initial cost for producing information through latest technology is expensive but the same becomes very cheap for reproducing. While reproducing information becomes cheap, there is a possibility for other to make it much cheaper by just copying the stuff and make their initial cost of generating the cheapest. This has created the need for having a copyright and establishes some form of private ownership for the information thus produced.

The United States government has authorised the congress to provide copyrights to the authors and inventors in the field of science, arts and technology. In the case of digital information these guidelines, policies and rules are not clear to manage the intellectual property. With the use of internet and the vulnerability of digital information to be copied and transmitted over internet making it very difficult to trace it world wide and control the intellectual property rights.

Internet has proven to be a giant copying machine challenging the Information Technology community to control its misuse. The producers of the information have very little probability of recovering their cost of producing the information which have been copied and sold out legitimately. Especially those published through web content needs to have some mechanism to avoid copying and reproducing in various other formats.

Versioning of the information might create some difficulty for others to copy and follow up. There has been a considerable effort to enforce all agencies involved in handling digital information with policies, guidelines and framework to maintain integrity of the ownership of the digital information.

Information Strategy for Business Networks

The world is changing towards better communication setup, state of the art information technology with a wide variety of options for small, medium and large scale business vendors. These business models have sidelined the conventional business methodologies and it is time for the government to adopt a framework to provide guidance, monitor the growing business and control them with business policies. Businesses which could follow the guidelines and accept these policies have flourished and the others went into problems.

Economic reconstruction has been possible with the advent of information world comprising of software and hardware designed to produce the necessary information required to manage the business process. Digital information refers to any information that can be represented in terms of series of digital bits which can be handled by digital devices for transmitting, receiving and processing to generate meaningful information.

The information thus obtained can be of different value to different domains like entertainment, business, sports, finance and many more. But each of these domains has different strategies to adopt the information technology. The infrastructure for such a technology is generally costly but involves cheap navigational cost. Therefore it depends on the domain to utilize the technology for generating profit or improvising the business process.

Most of the organisations either a high-tech manufacturing unit or a service industry, are considering some methodology of re-engineering their business process to establish information technology infrastructure to meet this new competitive world of technology. Focus on the staff training, development and support to build information technology skill and competencies and to enhance in-depth problem solving thereby increasing the value of implementing the information technology infrastructure.

Recent improvements in the information technology has changed the way organisations conduct business. Companies slash their expenditure with the help of real-time communication devices, availability of internet and implementing latest business models like distributed network and trading hubs. Yet many business organisations lack to achieve the optimum due to lack of proportion strategies for implementing IT infrastructure.

All the projects, systems and organisational practices should correspond to the value of the technology. This can be achieved through a System Development Life Cycle model which enhances the intended life span on the use of information technology infrastructure.

Strategic utilisation of Information Technology involves business oriented approach to use the features of information technology. There is a need to adopt a framework to maximise the use of Information technology assets. The use of information systems should reshape the strategy of the organisation and culture. The methods for embedding the information technology into the existing business process needs to be identified so as to achieve required change in the structure and culture of the organisation.

The organisation roles and responsibilities needs to be redefined matching with the information strategy. Encourage activities on research and development on the implementation and maintenance issues of Information Technology in the business. The protocol for data communication and network services needs to be identified. Information strategy should also account for work group activities.

Online Virtual Business Network

What is virtual business network?

Business and commerce, right from the ancient days, depended a lot on the physical representation of the business and the physical identity of the customers and other collaborators. Most of the business dealings were done person to person, face to face. After the invention of telephony, the dependence on physical identity for business transactions came down to some extent. However, the technological revolution in the field of Internet in this era has lead to the coining of a new term Virtual Business Network.

Virtual Business Network can be defined as a business that does not have a physical identity and operated entirely online on the world wide web. All identity and recognition issues of a business are done through secure electronic identification and validation process. Some businesses on the internet are even run from home with all the employees operating online from remote parts of the world. The earlier myth of needing huge financial investment, assets, workforce and infrastructure is gone with the advent of Virtual Business Networks. The awareness among customers about using the internet to find and procure services and products from their home is growing at a rapid rate.

Moreover, the reach of a customer is global in the sense that the customer can buy any product or service from any where in the world. If a business projects itself on the web through good quality web services and portfolio, it is likely to gain the confidence and get a huge international and national customer base. The entire business world realises this opportunity and also the importance of implementing the change over to virtual networking at the earliest.

What are the advantages of virtual business networking?

The first and foremost advantage of Virtual Business Networking is the ease with which it can be planned and implemented. There is little or no financial burden on implementing these changes to go online. All activities for performing business transactions such as strategic alliances, sales, joint ventures, advertising, marketing, HR management, knowledge development and sharing, business promotion etc. can be performed online. With experienced and skilled workers available online, there will be no need to set up a team and provide training.

With no major financial investment, associated with venturing into networking is very less. Also, the need for travelling through congested traffic to office or to travel across the globe for a business meeting is not necessary anymore. Network meeting using internet telephony or videophones is a fast growing trend. Telecommuting is another new word coined with the introduction of virtual business networks. Employees can do their work from home by logging on to the internet and at their own time.

With introduction of secure online financial transactions and electronic money, the virtual business networks have the unique advantage of making or getting payments across the globe in no time. With improved authentication and secure identification technologies, the virtual business networks no longer have the worry to identify their global customers anymore.

The global reach which the virtual business networking provides gives increasing opportunities to expanding a business nearly every day. With new contacts, affiliations, referrals and growing customer awareness, the virtual business network lays the path for success of a business right from the moment the business begins this venture.

Where to look for opportunities?

The first step is to formulate a profile for the business and the vision and goals associated with it. The next step is to start the process of building up an online virtual network of friends, affiliates and business seekers. There are several online communities, which apart from giving social networking, also help in promoting an online business. Some communities like the Linkedin, Xing, ZoomInfo, and Ecademy have grown in numbers and also helped the growth of number of virtual businesses.

A search on the web on the available business networks, community networks or other personal networks will help in deciding the most appropriate network suitable to a particular business. A targeted customer base can then be built using the links and referrals available online.

The second method involves setting up a network infrastructure and hosting a website with details about the services the business offers. A forum and business specific network can also be hosted in order to get more information about what the customers actually want. The data mining solutions help in understanding the market dynamics and the way customers respond to a product. With this added on information, the business can fine tune their marketing and pricing strategy to gain success online.

Tips to succeed in Virtual Business Networks

The first tip to being successful is the first impression a business creates. An appropriate, professional profile will aid in creating a good first impression. A profile which is attractive will bring good connections. The profile also aids in people get sufficient information about the business and to judge the outcome of forming a connection.

The next key aspect is to define a vision and goal which your business has. Similarity in vision and goal will attract like minded and similar businesses together as a strong tightly knit network. The next important aspect for success is to participate and share knowledge with other members in the network.

The more you share your knowledge, the more your business reputation builds. Keep a watch for good opportunities and never agree to a deal in which the business goals are not met. Maintaining the right focus is the key to success of a business in the virtual world. The more the time a business devotes online, the more the popularity it gains. Also the earlier a business adopts new strategies and online presence, the more will be its customer base and business relations. By associating with a popular non-profit cause during the early stages in the virtual world, a business can gain a lot of popularity and reliability.

Providing free consultation services in the core area of the business is one of these techniques. This also helps to establish the competency of the business in the core area. Instead aiming at all the customers, identifying a potential customer group and dealing with their needs will be a great advantage during the initial phases. A constant presence in the virtual world is just as essential as the first step of entering it. Long absences and lack of consistency will greatly hamper the reliability profile of a business.

Agility in Virtual Business Networks

Agility means responding to rapid changes and continuous change management. With the rapid economic changes and unexpected market behaviour, the virtual business networks have to adapt themselves to be able to respond in a timely and fast manner. Therefore agility provides the virtual business networks the ability to minimise losses and also as a risk deterrent. Agility can also be thought of as flexibility. The traditional businesses are more rigid in formulating a project flow and sticking to the plan till its completion.

Agility in the view point of business networks means the flexibility in incorporating changes during the execution of a long term project. This is the latest trend among the business network communities. This article will bring out the salient features of agility, its need and applicability in business networks.

Need for Agility

Agility is an important factor in case of projects that run into several years. It is not possible to forecast accurately about the risk factors and problems associated with such long term projects. The research and development programmes for the defense sector are the best example for such projects. The business networks realised the requirement of formulating and re-designing their supply chain process to provide for such rapid change request and adaptability. Based on research for several years, the new model of Agile Business network principles have been introduced. Hence Agility factor is considered as a strategic success tool. In order to evaluate the agility strategy considerable amount of time is required.

Factors Affecting Agility

To incorporate agility in business networks, it is important to understand the factors which affect its implementation in the business networks. There are other factors which contribute to the success in coordination with agility in a business network. The factors that are essential to be considered before adopting agility strategies in a business network are described below.

1. **Social factors**

   Social dynamics play a major role in determining the influence on agility of a business network. This is because most of the networks are formed with social and cultural interests in small regions around the world. Adopting a radical and new principle is considered risky and hence there is great resistance causing direct influence on the agility of the business network.

2. **Cultural Paradigms**

   The next important factor that affects agility is the cultural paradigms. These are age old policies and conventions followed for years by the members of a business network. In certain cases these paradigms are nation wide, and are accepted by the major business networks and vary from country to country.

3. **Management Metrics**

   Agility requires accurate results produced through analysis and management metrics. The factor of management metrics relies on accurate data for formulating metrics and measures which provide indication of the success of a particular business network model or process flow. Early detection of problems will lead to corrective action and prevent major disasters.

4. **Common Principles**

   The key factor that influences the agility in a business network is the formulation and adoption of a unified objective and goal. This involves a thorough study of the individual member businesses or companies of the business network and analysis to work out the unified vision acceptable by all the members.

Differentiating Agility

Before taking steps to incorporate agility in the business networks, there is a need to thoroughly understand the implications and effort involved. Implementing agility in a business network needs a lot of effort and time. The process of estimating and analysis in a business network after adopting strategies for agility is very complex and different from other e-commerce estimation and assessment techniques.

The costing and performance estimation in agility are different from the normal static e-commerce costing and ERP strategies. Flexibility is key factor which is applied to each and every assessment techniques applied for performance assessment in agile business networks. A new approach is required for formulating the process flow and how supply chains are maintained in an agile environment.

There is also requirement to adopt parallel lines simultaneously and estimate the progress of each line accurately to determine the performance metrics. These performance metrics can give the ability to predict the future course of action and expected results in following a particular process model. If problems are detected during the progress of a particular process work flow, alternative or the parallel line can continue to earn the revenue and compensate for the losses incurred in the failed process lines. This ensures good success rates and also reduces the risk of failure in long term projects in general.

Therefore a correct understanding of agility is mandatory for defining strategies based on agility in the collaborative business networks. The correct understanding of agility will also aid in formulating the optimum strategies for achieving good success estimates on long term project.

Tools for Agile Business Networks

Agility is very complex factor in a business network. Since the agile strategies are very difficult to formulate and also to assess, specialised software tools and methods have been devised to help the agile business networks to take advantage of the agility principle. These tools help in clearly defining the Infrastructure Elements and their impact on the agile business networks. The study on these infrastructure elements leads to creating the Infrastructure Observations and highlighting the key result areas and critical processes that need to be guarded.

The tools also formulate a set of Best Agile Practice methodologies for the practitioners to follow. The best agile practices are dependent heavily on the network hierarchy and hence there is a need to adopt these best practices on case to case basis instead of blindly following them. The next important aspect in an agile business network is the heavy reliance on the Information Theory aspects.

Secure and accurate communication and information flow mechanisms need to be adopted for successful implementation of agility in business networks. This requires a thorough study of the existing information flow process in the business network. The results of the study can be analysed using the mathematical tools for determining the changes required to adopt the existing information infrastructure to agile business network environment. There are several tools and software which are aimed at measuring and assessing performance through Metrics.

Smart Business Networks

Smart Business network is a creative way of doing business establishing a strong link to achieve effective results better than the conventional business. The word smart has been coined to the terminology not only referring to the literal meaning of smartness but also indicates doing business with a technological approach to produce different and better outcomes.

This business methodology adopts strategy to enhance the utilisation of communication technology and network systems. Smart Business Network can be considered as the linking nodes comprising of organisational. These nodes are linked to each other using a latest communication technology creating lines between various nodes involved in the business. All the nodes connected are working towards a common target and endeavour to synchronise efforts to achieve the target of the smart business network.

Most important aspect of setting up this business is long lasting, always working together with an effective output to the organisational goals. The linking may be fully looped with all the nodes of the organisation or it might adopt a hierarchical set up depending on the situation and best combination available. A chain in a network is connected exactly from one to another.

If there are suppliers in the network and certain nodes are earmarked as the customer to the supplier, then the concept of supply chain management is adopted. In general the customers are linked upwards towards the suppliers in the supply chain management. Smart business network is adaptable to situations, dynamic and has the ability to get linked easily and delinked quickly as possible.

Features of Smart Business Network

Presently smart business network is not a reality in the business world, researcher are maximizing their efforts to implement Smart Business Network. This business is a coordinated business with the features of alertness, vigorous established with adequate network structures and networking process.

This business technology utilises the benefits of innovative business to generate economic rents. The set up of Wal-Mart firm is an example describing some of the features of a small business network.

In this company they have incorporated Radio Frequency Identification (RFID) technology to track and trace their products Smart Business Network also has a unique business operating system which is responsible for coordinating the process among the nodes on network. The business has embedded logic of this operating system. Some of the manufacturing industries catching business process logic in the industry wide repositories which are shared via intranet and extranet of the company.

This business technology also offers the government to go for e-governance providing a user-friendly interface to both citizens as well as businessman. Transport and logistics companies have effective solution using smart business network to get quick online information on the product location and many more real-time information simplifying the business process. The other features of the smart business network include the following:

(a) It comprises of qualified suppliers and customers.

(b) Smartness of the business remains comparative, time-bound and suited to situation.

(c) Competitive Business coping up with the changing trends to manage the opposition in the business.

(d) Linked nodes in the smart business network have compatible goals.

(e) Communicating in novel way.

(f) Sustainable for a longer period.

(g) Adopts coordinated business process.

Implementing Smart Business Network

Organisations interested in implementing Smart Business Network needs to understand the basic road map for establishing the smart business network or reorienting their current business process towards smart business process. The first step is to identify the company who can provide support for installing an IT infrastructure or a network infrastructure according to the target and smart business process requirements defined by the company.

After identifying the service provider the next step is to analyse the management cost and improvement in the productivity of the proposed project. In general there has been reduction in the cost for voice and data communication experienced by the companies without having the smart business network environment. Typical implementation of a Smart Business Network would have the following:

(a) Managed Service Provider

(b) Internet

(c) Integrated service router

(d) Other network devices like switch, hub, routers, and application and file servers.

(e) The client side or the employee side would have a workstation, unified IP phone, facility for instant messaging, access to web based applications, company hosted e-mail services. In special cases companies would also provide a secured Wireless Access Point in the network for executive level personnel in the company.

(f) With IP communication the system has not only overcome the cost of public toll pass but also enhanced the network security using private links

(g) The set up can also be integrated with a Customer Relationship Management (CRM) software giving productivity enhancement features including pop-us, call tracking click to dial and many more features.

Managing Smart Business Network

The major challenges foreseen in managing the smart business network are structure of the network, adopted, monitoring and process used for negotiation and the Information Technology enabled incorporation. The following points need to be considered for managing a smart business network.

(a) The core business process should identify the strong and weak ties with their partners against their design, source, logistics structure, distribution system and after sales service. The players in the network should have the ability to interact in plug and play mode and have the abilities for dynamic negotiation.

(b) Policies on managing the agency conflicts and intellectual property should be well defined.

(c) The process of Information sharing among the partners in the SBN partners to coordinate their distributed as well as interdependent activities has to be considered before implementing Smart Business Network.

(d) The coordination process should also include the ability to convert the user requirement into product or service specifications and convert the specifications into items or production tasks.

(e) Linking of knowledge resource over wide geographical areas of the organisation.

(f) Incorporation of effective monitoring mechanism to control the various activities happening in the business network.

(g) The system should be long term predictable and has the ability to react to changing situations.

(h) The network should be able to identify the status of the member new entries and old member.

(i) The system should be designed to implement restructuring any portion of the network as per the changing requirement so as to establish alliances and promote effective as well as timely communication of information among the partners.

Internationalising a Business Network

Traditionally, only big enterprises and companies had the financial strength to become multinational firms. In the present era of information technology, small businesses and medium scale businesses have joined together from small business networks. The internet and the world wide web have brought the extremes of the earth closer through its rapid communication features.

The small business networks have taken full advantage of these technological innovations and are now able to compete with the multinational firms in the global market. Some of these business networks come from economically backward countries, some from the developing economies and others from the developed countries.

Hence competition is very tough and a pricing war takes immense proportions in the international perspective. Along with internationalisation and globalisation, several new studies and analysis has been conducted on international business.

Specialised reports in specific areas such as marketing, finance and management are also available. There are also research papers available on managing international business relationship. This article focuses on bringing out these aspects which will help in international business network development.

Managing Alliances

Alliances form the key part of any international business network. In general the control and coordination of these alliances is a very difficult and complex issue. The top management in this international business network formulates business strategies taking into consideration that all alliances will be able to implement it.

Moreover the international business management techniques are very essential in managing a lasting relationship with its international alliances. These alliances are empowered to take a wide array of decisions so as to complement the overall strategy of the business network. There are certain aspects and factors which greatly influence the international business networks to manage their alliances. These factors are discussed below:

1. **Regional factors**

   Different regions of the world follow different norms in business dealings. The alliances need to orient towards their business network and develop new methodologies in business dealings. The flexibility and adaptability of these foreign firms is an essential factor in overcoming the regional barriers and performing well in the international business networks.

2. **Social factors**

   Social dynamics play a major role in determining the influence on internationalisation of a business network. Most of the networks are formed with social and cultural interests in small regions around the world and they have common principles that unite them. When an alliance joins an international business network, there is a need to adopt radical and new principles which is generally considered risky and hence there is great resistance causing direct influence on the internationalisation of the business network.

3. **Cultural Factors**

   The next important factor that affects internationalisation is the cultural factor. These are age old policies and conventions followed for years by the members of a business network in a particular region in coordination with the cultural ethos of the region. In certain cases these paradigms are nation wide, and are accepted by the major business networks and vary from country to country. So when an international alliance is formed, these cultural aspects play an important role in the effectiveness of the internationalisation process.

4. **Religious Factors**

   The religious factors also play a very important and essential part in international business. Religious factors decide on the cohesiveness of a business in a network. However, these aspects are now being tackled with promoting the sole aim of success in the international ventures and mutual respect of each others religious aspects.

5. **International Management**

   Businesses thrive on the basis of accurate results produced through analysis and management metrics.

Management metrics and strategies rely heavily on the timely and accurate data obtained from the business network. Managing information flow in an international arena is a very complex process and forms a vital factor in managing the alliances.

International Business Networks Regulations

The formulation of legal agreements and licensing is the most complicated process in the effort to internationalisation of the business network. Each country defines its own policy for foreign alliances and collaborations. The government laws of the countries differ in many aspects.

The financial regulations, trade policies and international cooperation define the regulations which are necessary to be adopted for creating alliances with foreign country businesses. These rules also define the limits and licensing rules that need to be adopted.

Agreements on intellectual property rights and knowledge transfer are also essential to be considered in adding foreign alliances with the business networks.

The rules are also varied and differ from country to country. Problem arises when two different alliances from two different countries join a major business network.

In such cases, even though both the alliances need to be treated equal, the treaties and agreements between them and the business networks will differ.

Defining strategies to alleviate such differences will be very complex process. But once both alliances are made to agree on the common principles and rules of the business network, the possibility of successful collaboration and coordination is achieved.

International Consultancy

There are several firms which offer consultancy in the aspects of internationalising the various business networks. These consultancy services provide the necessary knowledge base about probable alliances, the problems that may come up in such alliances, benefits associates with the alliances, and also the cost effectiveness of the alliances.

This information is very vital for companies and business networks to work out feasible solutions and analyse the risk factors associated in such ventures.

The business can also take help from these consultancy firms to perform feasibility study and analysis on the legal and licensing aspects of internationalisation of their business network.

The specialised, country specific consultancy agencies are also available. These agencies maintain an up to date legal policies and trade policies and their interpretation specific to various regions of the world.

Certain consultancy services also provide guidance and advice to the business networks in establishing secure and effective alliance ties within the regional regulations and limitations.

Special country specific trade shows are also avenues where these consultancy services show case their expertise and knowledge, base in providing consultancy solutions to the business networks planning to expand to international markets.

Freelancer Opportunities in Business Networks

Freelancing means the process through which individual work from home. The freelancers earn money by providing expertise and skills to customers in the virtual business networks and internet. The unique requirement of a freelancer to be successful in the virtual word is the freelancer's innovative talent, expertise, creativity and special skill. Mostly the jobs are paid on per project basis and payment depends on the type and extent of services and work required.

Several small businesses have also adopted the concept of employing virtual employees on the internet because of shortage of work force or to reduce cost of hiring permanent employees. Freelancers suit best to take on these virtual employee jobs through the internet. The freelancers can also be looked upon as independent contractors who bid on project by project basis and take on the job from home.

In most cases the freelancer has to negotiate project terms and conditions with the customers themselves. After completing one project successfully the freelancer starts to search for other projects. But there is also a possibility for freelancers to take on more than one project from several different clients at the same time. In some cases the freelancers generate reports, special research papers and other services which they sell to customers on the internet.

This freelancer job can also be looked upon as a small home based business. The individuals without a job, retired individuals, house wives, students and handicapped individuals can all start on this new venture with no financial requirement to start up at all.

Freelancer Jobs

The freelancer projects and jobs are available from small business networks and social networks. The projects or work is not regular in nature and are mostly short term and ad hoc jobs. The Business networks also look for freelancers when the workload is high and there is need for more staff. In this case also the jobs and projects are short term and temporary. The most common freelancer job opportunities on the internet are listed and described below.

1. **Web Programming**

   With the boom in internet Business, several small Businesses and virtual Business network are in need of creating websites and services. This requirement is of short duration and the businesses cannot afford to employ a permanent web development staff. Hence they seek freelance web programmers to avail their special expertise in a certain area of web programming arena.

2. **Web Journalism**

   The online magazines and newspapers need to publish live, fresh news for their websites to be successful. Moreover, they need information from across the world. To employ a global staff, a lot of financial investment is needed. So these websites hire freelancers from all over the world to work on part time basis.

3. **Web Content Writing**

   With the growing number of websites and need for continuously posting fresh content so as to maintain their Business information, small Business look for freelancers to do market research and post articles on their websites.

4. **Web Consultancy**

   Specialists in the field of legal Business, technological experts and domain specialists are sought regularly by the small Business community for aiding them in projects. These are mostly high paid part time job opportunities in the virtual Business networks.

5. **Online Training**

   Small Businesses also cannot cater for specialist training staff. So they look for freelancers with the requisite skills and expertise to conduct training for their staff on project to project basis and on temporary basis.

6. **Marketing**

    This is the most common opportunity which the small Businesses offer on the internet. The companies and Businesses expect the freelancers to do the marketing through e-mail or web blogs. The payment is mostly based on the sales achieved by the freelancer and also in some cases part of the profit earned.

Essential Business Networking Techniques

Improve your business networking techniques and grow your business by expanding your contacts and building relationships with other people. Here you will find lots of networking information, great tips, essential tools and key networking advice to help you get the most out of networking and generate new business.

It's a fact - 70% on average of new business is gained through referrals or relationship marketing, and not only that it is one of the most cost-effective ways of building your business.

You may already have spent considerable time, effort and money on other marketing methods such as advertising or direct mailing with little or no return. Or perhaps you have tried cold-calling with little to show for your efforts leaving you feeling demoralised and no further forward.

Read on, follow tips and advice and you will soon have all the networking information you need to become a top networker and see your business grow.

Developing the "You" Factor

It's a fact, in business people buy people and they buy people that they know, like and trust. So, it stands to reason that if you are going to get the results you are looking for you need to be able to attract others to you and also compel them to find out more and to stick around to help you out and pass business and contacts your way.

So, how can you exploit the "people buy people" philosophy? Develop the "you" factor!

1. **Be authentic**

   Firstly, if a key criteria is about people getting to know, like and trust you then it follows that you have to be genuine and authentic - others will soon see through you if you aren't being genuine. Therefore you need to be yourself and learn to express your positive qualities.

   Ask yourself 'on a scale of 1-10' how authentic do I feel when I go out and network? Are you a 10 where you really are being yourself or do you feel that you are putting on one big act for the benefit of others? (because it certainly won't be for your benefit.)

   Often when people start networking they think they have to put on an act to give a good impression - but ask yourself - what is wrong with the 'real' you? If you then find that the 'real' you is so incongruent with the ethos of where you are networking then you might want to ask yourself whether you are networking in the right place.

   Consider also what you are wearing - do your clothes reflect your personality and the image you want to portray?

   If you are struggling to know who you really are you might want to spend some time reflecting on your values and what your strengths are.

2. **Discover your passions.**

   Think of those times when you have met people who are passionate about what they do and their sheer enthusiasm and passion has been infectious. People are naturally drawn towards passion in others whatever their passions may be and are far more likely to want to spend time in their company and help them.

Ask yourself how passionate you are about what you do. Remember you must remain authentic so you cannot fake passion, so if you do not feel passionate about what you do perhaps now is the time for discovering your true passions.

So how do you discover your passions - well, think of those times you have gained a real buzz from your work- what really gets you excited about what you do?

If you are struggling here then remember that if you network without that passion and enthusiasm your competitor will already have that advantage over you.

3. **Help others first**

   Effective networkers always aim to help others first. In some ways this may seem like a paradox to the principle of setting personal goals for networking but the principle of helping others does actually sit alongside your own goals.

   By helping others you will not only build up a deep sense of personal satisfaction you will also naturally build up a desire in others to help you in return. However, that desire to help must be genuine, and not merely an action to gain 'credit' with others for the future.

4. **Take responsibility**

   As an effective networker you must take responsibility for the results you get from networking. It is all too easy to blame others, whether it is others in a networking group for not bringing you the referrals you want or the organisers of a networking event for not bringing you the contacts you need. Read all these business networking tips but ultimately it is up to you to question what you need to do to get the results you want and remember, "people buy people"

Understand Building Relationships

A really important networking technique is relationship building. The generation of business through referral or 'positive recommendation' comes when people have come to know, like and trust you. Here are top tips for building successful business relationships:

KNOW

- Be able to succinctly describe the benefits of your service.
- If you can't describe them, then how can others?
- Be specific about the help you want - who do you want referrals to?
- How can someone recognise that someone else needs your service?
- How effective are your business cards – do they clearly convey what you do? Do you use both sides?
- Do you have effective promotional material that clearly conveys how you/your services are of value to others?

LIKE

- Help others first.
- Never criticise others.
- Provide written and verbal testimonials whenever possible.
- Be supportive to others when they need it.

TRUST

- Be authentic - don't try to be someone you are not - remember it is 'you' that is your unique selling point and people will see through an 'act'.
- Deliver your promises and exceed expectations with the service you provide.
- Be a good customer - pay on time.

Power networkers know that building relationships starts by helping others. Here are some networking tips for easy ways to help others.

1. **Take time to find out how you can help others**

   Listening is the highest form of respect you can show someone.

   - Show genuine interest in someone's business and find out
   - What services and benefits do they offer
   - What customers are they looking for
   - What contacts would be useful for them
   - How else can you help them

2. **Spot opportunities for others**

   Whether you are with friends and family or work colleagues listen to what problems they have. Do you know someone who can solve that problem for them, providing them with a business opportunity?

3. **Share your contacts with others**

   Be prepared to give names and contact details to those people you know like and trust.

4. **Make positive introductions**

   If you spot two people who could benefit from knowing each other make the effort to introduce each other.

When relationship building with your contacts use positive words such as 'Mary is the really great accountant I was talking to you about' or 'Peter is a real expert in building websites-he's really helped me get more business already.'

5. **'Warm up' leads**

   Ask your contact whether they may be contacted by the person whose services you are referring. This way you are warming up the lead and that person knows to expect a call.

6. **Provide testimonials**

   Testimonials are a great way of demonstrating that you have satisfied customers so think how grateful your suppliers will be if you voluntarily given them a written testimonial. Remember to provide an electronic copy so they can just copy and paste it for use on their website and marketing material.

7. **Give free**

   If someone has a problem be generous with any help and advice you can give which draws upon your area of expertise. This will not only show you are willing to help but also that you are an expert in this area.

8. **Return favours**

   Thank someone for any favours they have done for you and ask how you can help in return.

Business Networking Goals

Setting effective business networking goals are an absolute must if you are to get full value for your time and money from your business networking activities.

Have you ever

- turned up to an event without any clear purpose?

- wandered around aimlessly talking to just anyone who might be free?
- let conversations drift at the expense of meeting other people?
- not made full use of your time with the people you have spoken with?
- come away from any event thinking you could have made better use of your time and money?

If the answer is yes then you are not alone, so many of us at some point have fallen into one or more of these traps, wasting both time and money, all of which can be avoided if you take time out to prepare your business networking plan and set yourself clear goals at the outset.

If you set yourself clearly defined goals then you will not only use your time efficiently, you will get the results you are seeking. Clearly defined goals fixed clearly in your head will automatically guide you to spending your time in the best way for you.

The goal setting networking advice is:

- Decide what you must achieve to have made the event worthwhile e.g. is your objective to distribute your business cards to everyone attending, is it a fact-finding exercise, do you want to specifically talk to two or three people who you could form a strategic alliance with or do you want to speak with someone who could introduce you to a particular organisation?
- Be clear on who you want to talk to - if possible ask for a list of attendees, and decide who on the list you think it would be most useful to talk to.
- Think about what information you want to go away with.

- Think about what information you want to convey? (And always keep in mind networking is not about selling, it's about meeting people and building relationships so they will want to talk to you at a later date.)
- If the passing of referrals are an integral part of the event think about what specific introductions you are looking for and be prepared to ask for them.
- Consider what else you want to happen as a result of your attendance at the event?
- Finally, have a clear picture of your goal in your head and be positive about achieving it - think about how it will feel if you achieve it. Act as if you have already achieved the goal. The Law of Attraction says that your thoughts and feelings become reality!

Effective One to One Meetings

One to one meetings are all part of the business to business networking process and here's how to get the most out of this essential relationship building technique. In a roomful of people your goal is most likely to make contact with a number of people and to make an assessment as to whether it is worth developing a relationship further. If this is the case then you will most likely want to schedule time in private at a later date, to find out more about each other in more detail. Some tips to think about:

1. **Establish a clear purpose for your 1 to 1**

   To be useful both you and the other party need to understand why you are spending time together and what you will talk about. If you have only just met someone, a one on one is likely to be a further exploration of each other's business and how you can help each other. Don't dive straight in with a full pitch....remember the value in building relationships.

2. **Schedule in a specific time**

   Agree how long you will need to achieve your objectives-perhaps one hour will be enough to explore each others businesses, however two hours may be more appropriate if you have already spotted a number of areas to discuss. Either way make sure that you are both in agreement.

3. **Prepare an agenda**

   Depending on how formal you want your one to one to be will determine whether you want a written agenda. If it seems too formal for a chat over a cup of coffee at least verbally agree what you want to cover.

   A typical format may be:

   - discuss them and their business
   - discuss you and your business
   - explore areas of mutual interest
   - agree action

4. **Ask about their business first**

   Take the initiative and find out about the other person and their business first. Ask questions and listen carefully. This not only will make the other person feel good it will arm you with invaluable information to help you to tailor what you say about your business.

5. **Establish how you can help the other person**

   Remember one to ones are-an extension of the networking process and networking is about relationship building. If you show a genuine interest in the other person's needs and how you can help them, this is a great way of building up your relationship with them.

6. **Agree Action**

   At the end of your business to business meeting agree if any action is to be taken by either of you.

7. **Take Action**

   Now this is where so many business relationships fail before they even get started. Do ensure you follow up on any action you have agreed and particularly seek to help the other Person.

Asking the Right Questions

It's essential to master the skill of how to ask questions in the right way if you are going to build relationships with people, understand them and their businesses.

Here are some tips for helping you to ask questions in the right way when you are out networking so you really are making the most of your time talking with others.

1. **Getting a person to talk**

   As a rule asking open questions, questions which elicit more than one word answers will gain you more information. So asking questions beginning with 'who', 'what,' 'why,' 'where,' 'when,' 'how' and 'tell me about' are great to get the other person talking. This is more effective to get people talking than the' do you...,"are you...' questions which elicit a specific and usually one word response 'yes' or 'no.'

2. **At the beginning of a conversation ask questions that are easy & open**

   When you first meet someone it really is about building rapport with that person so don't be afraid to ask the simple and safe questions such as 'who else do you know here?' and 'where do you live?'

3. **Once you have started to build rapport progress to more business-related questions.**

   If you stick with just small talk it is unlikely you will achieve what you have come to this networking event for...to gain business contacts. So don't be afraid to move onto asking about the other person's business... what do they do, where are they based, what is their market?

4. **Established the other person's challenges and needs**

   One question that is so easy to ask which can reveal so much about the other persons' business and their current needs is 'what challenges do you currently face in your business?' Whether it is staffing needs, training needs, motivation needs, or problems with bad debts this question can uncover so many issues that this person faces which you can park in your mind for the future. Whilst it's not about diving in and saying' oh yes, I can help you with that' it is about having that information at a later date that will help determine whether you need to get to know this person further.

5. **Ask more specific questions to get more specific answers**

   Once you have built a level or rapport and built up a general understanding of the other person's business you can then ask more specific questions. 'Who exactly is your ideal client?' 'Where are your customers mainly based?'

6. **Ask closed questions to close down a conversation**

   Sometimes you will find yourself with someone who just won't stop talking so asking more closed questions rather than open questions could help stem the flow of conversation. So move away from the tell me more about' question to 'or 'have you been to one of these events before.'

If you are ready to move on from this person asking a question like 'would you like me to introduce you to...?' or 'I'm getting a bit hungry... shall we get some food?' are great ways to bring a conversation to an end politely.

7. **If the relationship is worth developing ask for a further one to one meeting**

   Clearly at a networking event it is highly unlikely that you are going to be able to build relationships with someone enough to then do business with them straightaway. In your initial conversations though by asking the right questions you may have established some common ground and potential opportunities to work with each other in the future.

   If this is the case it is about establishing whether the other person would like to talk further and have a one to one meeting where possibilities can be explored. So before you leave the event ensure you both have the same understanding by asking the following:

   - Would you like to talk further?
   - When would be a convenient time to call you to arrange a meeting?
   - How is your diary looking this month?
   - Shall we aim to arrange a meeting before the end of the month?

8. **Questions to avoid**

   The questions to avoid are ones that could be potentially sensitive such as 'are you married, do you have children, what are your politics/religious view, how much do you earn'. Ask questions like these and you won't build relationships, more likely you'll wreck them before they've even begun.

Effective Listening Tips

Why develop effective listening skills? Listening to what someone has to say is the highest level of respect you can show to anyone. Not only that, it just feels so great when someone takes time to listen to and show genuine interest in what you have to say that it is the basis of developing a relationship with that person.

Also by listening you have the opportunity to pick up valuable information that will help you establish what that other person's needs are, what contacts they have, what useful experience and expertise they have etc.

So, if you want to develop first class relationships with people have a look at these following tips to see how you can improve your own listening skills.

1. **Stop talking!**

   Yes the first step in listening to others is to stop talking yourself and give time for other people to talk. Maybe you are a natural talker and don't like empty silences, but this isn't an excuse for you to do all the talking.

2. **Effective listening means don't interrupt**

   Whilst your enthusiasm for what the other person is saying might prompt you to dive in with your own thoughts, hold back until they have finished talking. Recognise too that people process information differently so some people talk faster than others therefore, allow time for people to think between sentences.

3. **Look for common ground**

   To help you listen with genuine interest listen out for

common ground - how are their experiences be similar to your own, how can their expertise be useful to someone you know, who do you know in common?

4. **Listening for feelings and moods**

   Words alone do not give the full picture about what someone is saying. Their tone of voice and body language give away far more about a person's mood and feelings, so part and parcel of listening is also listening to the meaning behind someone's words and observing their body language.

5. **Show that you are listening**

   Not only should you listen attentively, it is also important for you to show that you are listening:

   - show you are listening verbally by using listening noises - 'uh. ..huh'. . .'ummmm.. .right'
   - use non-verbal signals such as nodding your head and maintaining eye contact with the speaker
   - reflect back what has been said. . . 'so you primarily do business with blue chip organisations?'
   - build on what has been said and ask further related questions . . .'so you have an accountancy firm... where is that based?'
   - show empathy.. .'it sounds like you've had a difficult time then...'

❑❑❑

4
Business Capabilities and Competencies

Business capabilities describe WHAT the business is doing to reach the business goals and objectives. Each business capability should have an input and it must generate value to the business. Although business capabilities can be used in business processes that describe HOW the business is doing daily work, business capabilities never deal with HOW (just WHAT). Each business capability might have corresponding business process that describes how the capability being done (people, data, events, decision points, capabilities and relations between all mentioned elements).

Business capabilities in hierarchal manner, starting form high level business functions and breaking them to low level functions. Some people tend to break business capabilities by organisation structure. Although this is very convenient easy way, it creates a twisted view of the business capabilities (usually because capabilities are cross organisation). In a hierarchal view of business capabilities low level capabilities could be duplicated and exist in several high level capabilities (Sometimes this scenario is bad sometimes it is good).

Business capabilities are a way to model your business, but they are also one of the best way to bridge between business and information technologies. To create the bridge we simply use business capabilities as a hook that we want to hang on all of the IT assets that we have.

In addition to hooking capabilities to IT assets we keep certain amount of properties for each capability. Keeping many properties might be very impressive, but always remember that you need to maintain the data that you entered as well. The trick here is to understand what it the purpose of your enterprise architecture work and to collect just the needed data for this purpose.

Common usage of business capabilities:

1. Create alignment between Business and IT
2. Enable creation of business oriented IT roadmaps
3. A tool that helps business improvement efforts
4. Services identification
5. What are the services that the business need
   - In the right level of granularity
   - To enable business agility
   - To implement by IT
6. Validation of vendor's packages to business needs

   One of the biggest advantage of business capabilities is that they required much less resources and effort to maintain, while bringing the same ROT for enterprise architecture as business processes will generate. Focusing on the what reduce significantly the amount of resources needed to maintain them.

Business capabilities effort can be spitted into 5 main steps:

- Initial collection of data. Collect all the data that you can by yourself and try to build first version of the business capabilities map and use it in the next step. The most common resources that you can get to build the map are:

- Job Description
- Internal procedures
- Business Reference Models
  - o SCOR
  - o VCOR
  - o SAP Business scenarios
- Interviews. After you have some starting point as a reference, start to interview business users to validate and change the map. This is iterative process that might take some time and usually involved usage of your soft skills.
  - o Don't come to interviews with empty hands! Use collected data to create initial model. Use them to facilitated interviews.
  - o Use Nylon cover and camera to take interviews comments and compare them
  - o Valid and augment initial map

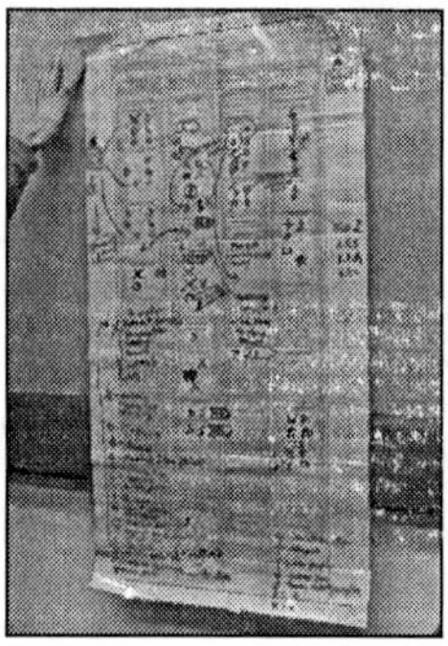

- Formal approve. If you can get CxO level approve you are on the right path to success. If not try to get any high level management approve, just make sure that business management participant.
- Relate IT to Business Capabilities. Ask business users to set what are the IT resources that they are using to carry on capability and to what extent IT assets are helping them. IT assets should include:
  - o Application
  - o Technology
  - o Services
- Relate business capabilities to Business objectives.

While low level capabilities mapped to IT, high level should be mapped to business objectives. Relating capabilities to business objectives will help us to understand what is the Wight of each capability from business point of view.

Business capabilities are very powerful both for business, information, applications and technology architecture. Once you went through the process of collecting them you have an important asset that will serve you as enterprise architect in most of your tasks. Business capabilities won't just help you in your tasks they will also give you much more time to do your work, because they demand much less resources for maintenance.

Business Competencies

Competencies refer to capabilities, abilities, skills, proficiencies, expertise and experience. There are two types of competencies-technical and non-technical. In terms of business competencies, we are focused on non-technical competencies often referred to as professional and personal skills. We also include both motivational values and behaviour as non-technical competencies because of their profound impact on job performance and satisfaction.

Technical Competencies

These are the skills and experiences that you can most often identify from an individual's resume (if speaking about a job candidate):

- ACHIEVEMENTS - results the candidate should be able to achieve in the job based on similar experiences in the past
- SKILLS - what the candidate should be able to specifically do such as launch a new brand into a certain channel
- KNOWLEDGE - educational background; what the

employee should know such as large account sales or marketing

- EXPERTISE - what the employee should have previously experienced arid become expert at such as managing field technicians in the oil and gas industry
- RELATIONSHIPS - colleagues, clients, peers, organisations with whom the employee should have a professional network

Technical competencies are easily verified and discussed. It's either they have then or they haven't. Technical competencies should always be verified.

Non-Technical Competencies

These are professional and personal skills and include both motivational values and behaviour. These competencies - more often than not — are the accelerators of performance or — if lacking in sufficient strength and quality - are the reason people fail to excel in jobs.

Think of it this way: two people, similar looks, stature, etc. Graduated from the same colleges and earned the same degrees with similar grades. They both go to work for Company X. One is a star; the other becomes dissatisfied, quits and goes on to another company. The differences between , these two people are non-technical competencies.

Examples of Non-Technical Competencies we Measure:

We measure over one hundred non-technical competencies. A few include:

- Accountability for others
- Analysis of data
- Competitiveness
- Empathetic outlook
- Personal relationships
- Correcting others

- Developing others
- Results orientation
- Concrete organisation
- Accurate listening
- Self esteem
- Job Ethics
- Role awareness
- Urgency
- Desire to lead
- Importance of knowledge / information
- Self-confidence

Importance of Non-Technical Competencies to Job Success

Personal and professional competencies provide a framework to manage organisational culture, core competency management, leadership development, and drive organisational performance. Assuming an employee possesses the required threshold technical competencies, non-technical competencies become the greatest determinants of employee performance. (We too often hire for skills and fire for attitude.) This is why so many companies are including benchmarking as a part of their hiring process and then comparing the competencies of candidates to the competency requirements of the job. And the way to understand candidate competencies is by using the right assessment tools that can accurately and reliably measure them.

Capabilities and Competencies

Capability-based strategies are based on the notion that internal resources and core competencies derived from distinctive capabilities provide the strategy platform that underlies a firm's long-term profitability. Evaluation of these capabilities begins with a company capability profile, which examines a company's strengths and weaknesses in four key areas:

- managerial
- marketing
- financial
- technical

Then a SWOT analysis (Strengths, Weaknesses, Opportunities, and Threats analysis) is carried out to determine whether the company has the strengths necessary to deal with the specific forces in the external environment. This analysis enables managers to identify:

- external threats and opportunities, and
- distinct competencies that can ward off the threats and compensate for weaknesses.

The picture identified by the SWOT analysis helps to suggest which type of strategy, or strategic thrust the firm should use to gain competitive advantage.

Here are four principles that serve as guidelines to achieving capability-based competition:

- Corporate strategy does not depend on products or markets but on business processes.
- Key strategic processes are needed to consistently provide superior value to the customer.
- Investment is made in capability, not functions or SBUs.
- The CEO must champion the capability-based strategy.

Capability-based strategies, sometimes referred to as the resource-based view of the firm, are determined by (a) those internal resources and capabilities that provide the platform for the firm's strategy and (b) those resources and capabilities that are the primary source of profit for the firm. A key management function is to identify what resource gaps need to be filed in order to maintain a competitive edge where these capabilities are required.

Several levels can be established in defining the firm's overall strategy platform (see figure).

At the bottom of the pyramid are the basic resources a firm has compiled over time. They can be categorised as technical factors, competitive factors, managerial factors, and financial factors.

Core competencies can be defined as the unique combination of the resources and experiences of a particular firm. It takes time to build these core competencies and they are difficult to imitate. Critical to sustaining these core competencies are their:

1. **Durability-**

   Their life span is longer than individual product or technology life-cycles, as are the life spans of resources used to generate them, including people.

2. **Intransparency-**

   It is difficult for competitors to imitate these competencies quickly.

3. **Immobility-**

   These capabilities and resources are difficult to transfer.

❑❑❑

5
Marketing Strategy

A marketing strategy is a process that can allow an organisation to concentrate its limited resources on the greatest opportunities to increase sales and achieve a sustainable competitive advantage. A marketing strategy should be centred on the key concept that-customer satisfaction is the main goal.

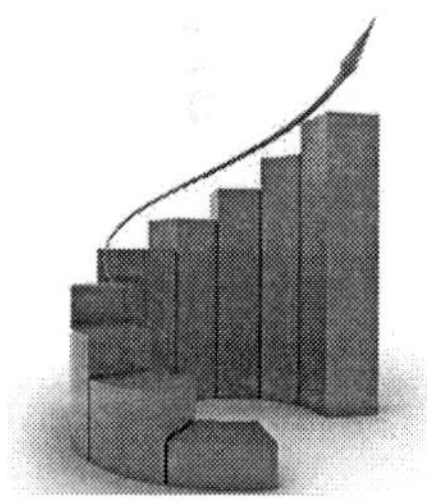

The marketing concept of building an organisation around the profitable satisfaction of customer needs has helped firms to achieve success in high-growth, moderately competitive markets. However, to be successful in markets in which economic growth has levelled and in which there exist many competitors who follow the marketing concept a well developed marketing strategy is required. Such a strategy considers a portfolio of products and takes into account the anticipated moves of competitors in the market.

A marketing strategy serves as the foundation of a marketing plan. A marketing plan contains a list of specific actions required to successfully implement a specific marketing strategy. An example of marketing strategy is as follows: "Use a low cost product to attract consumers. Once our organisation, via our low cost product, has established a relationship with consumers, our organisation will sell additional, higher-margin products and services that enhance the consumer's interaction with the low-cost product or service."

A strategy is different than a tactic. While it is possible to write a tactical marketing plan without a sound, well-considered strategy, it is not recommended. Without a sound marketing strategy, a marketing plan has no foundation. Marketing strategies serve as the fundamental underpinning of marketing plans designed to reach marketing objectives. It is important that these objectives have measurable results.

A good marketing strategy should integrate an organisation's marketing goals, policies, and action sequences (tactics) into a cohesive whole. The objective of a marketing strategy is to provide a foundation from which a tactical plan is developed. This allows the organisation to carry out its mission effectively and efficiently. A key component of marketing strategy is often to keep marketing in line with a company's overarching mission statement.

Mission statement is a brief written statement purpose of a company or organisation. Ideally, a mission statement guides the actions of the organisation, spells out its overall goal, provides a sense of direction, and guides decision making for all levels of management.

One used the following techniques to device the Marketing Strategy for the product/service:

- Segmentation
- Positioning
- Targeting

Segmentation

Market segmentation is the process in marketing of grouping a market (i.e. customers) into smaller subgroups. This is not something that is arbitrarily imposed on society: it is derived from the recognition that the total market is often made up of submarkets (called 'segments'). These segments are homogeneous within (i.e. people in the segment are similar to each other in their attitudes about certain variables). Because of this intra-group similarity, they are likely to respond somewhat similarly to a given marketing strategy. That is, they are likely to have similar feeling and ideas about a marketing mix comprised of a given product or service, sold at a given price, distributed in a certain way, and promoted in a certain way.

Market segmentation is widely defined as being a complex process consisting in two main phases:

- Identification of broad, large markets
- Segmentation of these markets in order to select the most appropriate target markets and develop Marketing mixes accordingly.

Everyone within the Marketing world knows and speaks of segmentation yet not many truly understand its underlying mechanics, thus failure is just around the corner. What cause this? It has been documented that most marketers fail the segmentation exam and start with a narrow mind and a bunch of misconceptions such as "all teenagers are rebels", "all elderly women buy the same cosmetics brands" and so on. There are many dimensions to be considered, and uncovering them is certainly an exercise of creativity.

Identify and Name the Broad Market

You have to have figured out by this moment what broad market your business aims at. If your company is already on a market, this can be a starting point; more options are available for a new business but resources would normally be a little limited.

The biggest challenge is to find the right balance for your business: use your experience, knowledge and common sense to estimate if the market you have just identified earlier is not too narrow or too broad for you.

Identify and make an Inventory of Potential Customers' Needs

This step pushes the creativity challenge even farther, since it can be compared to a brainstorming session.

What you have to figure out is what needs the consumers from the broad market identified earlier might have. The more possible needs you can come up with, the better.

Got yourself stuck in this stage of segmentation? Try to put yourself into the shoes of your potential customers: why would they buy your product, what could possibly trigger a buying decision? Answering these questions can help you list most needs of potential customers on a given product market.

Formulate Narrower Markets

Try to form sub-markets around what you would call your "typical customer", then aggregate similar people into this segment, on the condition to be able to satisfy their needs using the same Marketing mix. Start building a column with dimensions of the major need you try to cover: this will make it easier for you to decide if a given person should be included in the first segment or you should form a new segment. Also create a list of people-related features, demographics included, for each narrow market you form-a further step will ask you to name them.

There is no exact formula on how to form narrow markets: use your best judgement and experience. Do not avoid asking opinions even from non-Marketing professionals, as different people can have different opinions and you can usually count on at least those items most people agree on.

Identify the Determining Dimensions

Carefully review the list resulted form the previous step. You should have by now a list of need dimensions for each market segment: try to identify those that carry a determining power.

Reviewing the needs and attitudes of those you included within each market segment can help you figure out the determining dimensions.

Name Possible Segment Markets

You have identified the determining dimensions of your market segments, now review them one by one and give them an appropriate name.

A good way of naming these markets is to rely on the most important determining dimension.

Evaluate the Behaviour of Market Segments

Once you are done naming each market segment, allow time to consider what other aspects you know about them. It is important for a market to understand marketer behaviour and what triggers it. You might notice that, while most segments have similar needs, they're still different needs: understanding the difference had acting upon it is the key to achieve success using competitive offerings.

Estimate the Size of each Market Segment

Each segment identified, named and studied during the previous stages should finally be given an estimate size, even if, for lack of data, it is only a rough estimate.

Positioning

Simply, positioning is how your target market defines you in relation to your competitors. A good position is:

1. What makes you unique
2. This is considered a benefit by your target market

Both of these conditions are necessary for a good positioning. So what if you are the only red-haired singer who only knows how to play a G minor chord? Does your target market consider this a good thing?

Positioning is important because you are competing with all the noise out there competing for your potential fans attention. If you can stand out with a unique benefit, you have a chance at getting their attention.

It is important to understand your product from the customers point of view relative to the competition.

Environment

In order to begin positioning a product, two questions need to be answered:

1. What is our marketing environment?
2. What is our competitive advantage?

The marketing environment is the external environment. Some things to consider:

- How is the market now satisfying the need your software satisfies?
- What are the switching costs for potential users for your market?
- What are the positions of the competition?

The competitive advantage is an internal question. What do you have that gives you advantage over your competitors. Some things to consider:

- Is your company small and flexible?
- Do you offer low cost and high quality?
- Does your product offer unique benefits?
- Are you the first on the market with this product (First mover advantage)?

Positioning Strategies

There are seven positioning strategies that can be pursued:

1. Product Attributes: What are the specific product attributes?
2. Benefits: What are the benefits to the customers?
3. Usage Occasions: When / how can the product be used?
4. Users: Identify a class of users.
5. Against a Competitor: Positioned directly against a competitor.
6. Away from a Competitor: Positioned away from competitor.
7. Product Classes: Compared to different classes of products.

Targeting

Target Marketing involves breaking a market into segments and then concentrating your marketing efforts on one or a few key segments.

Target marketing can be the key to a small business's success. The beauty of target marketing is that it makes the promotion, pricing and distribution of your products and/ or services easier and more cost-effective. Target marketing provides a focus to all of your marketing activities.

So if, for instance, I open a catering business offering catering services in the client's home, instead of advertising with a newspaper insert that goes out to everyone, I could target my market with a direct mail campaign that went only to particular residents.

While market segmentation can be done in many ways, depending on how you want to slice up the pie, three of the most common types are:

1. Geographic segmentation - based on location such as home addresses;
2. Demographic segmentation - based on measurable statistics, such as age or income;
3. Psychographic segmentation - based on lifestyle preferences, such as being urban dwellers or pet lovers.

Tactics and Actions

A marketing strategy can serve as the foundation of a marketing plan. A marketing plan contains a set of specific actions required to successfully implement a marketing strategy. For example: "Use a low cost product to attract consumers. Once our organisation, via our low cost product, has established a relationship with consumers, our organisation will sell additional, higher-margin products and services that enhance the consumer's interaction with the low-cost product or service."

A strategy consists of a well thought out series of tactics to make a marketing plan more effective. Marketing strategies serve as the fundamental underpinning of marketing plans designed to fill market needs and reach marketing objectives. Plans and objectives are generally tested for measurable results.

A marketing strategy often integrates an organisation's marketing goals, policies, and action sequences (tactics) into a cohesive whole. Similarly, the various strands of the strategy, which might include advertising, channel marketing, internet marketing, promotion and public relations, can be orchestrated. Many companies cascade a strategy throughout an organisation, by creating strategy tactics that then become strategy goals for the next level or group. Each one group is expected to take that strategy goal and develop a set of tactics to achieve that goal. This is why it is important to make each strategy goal measurable. Marketing strategies are dynamic and interactive. They are partially planned and partially unplanned.

Types of Strategies

Marketing strategies may differ depending on the unique situation of the individual business. However there are a number of ways of categorising some generic strategies. A brief description of the most common categorising schemes is presented below:

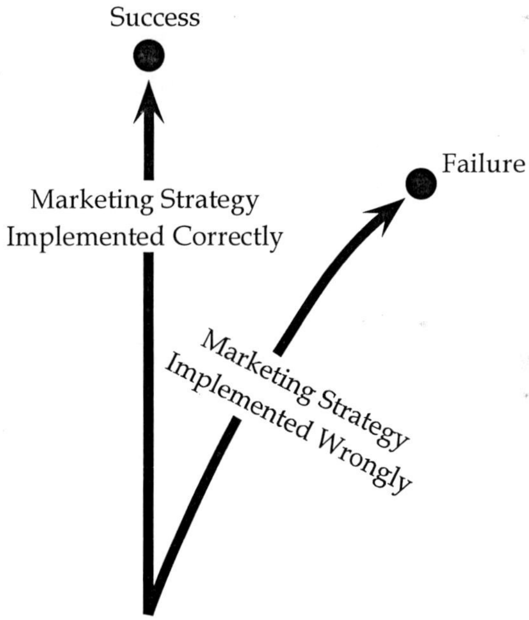

1. **Strategies based on market dominance -**

   In this scheme, firms are classified based on their market share or dominance of an industry. Typically there are three types of market dominance strategies:

   - Leader
   - Challenger
   - Follower

2. **Porter generic strategies-**

   Strategy on the dimensions of strategic scope and strategic strength. Strategic scope refers to the market penetration while strategic strength refers to the firm's sustainable competitive advantage.

   - Product differentiation
   - Market segmentation

3. **Innovation strategies-**

   This deals with the firm's rate of the new product development and business model innovation. It asks whether the company is on the cutting edge of technology and business innovation. There are three types:

   - Pioneers
   - Close followers
   - Late followers

4. **Growth strategies-**

   In this scheme we ask the question, "How should the firm grow?". There are a number of different ways of answering that question, but the most common gives four answers:

   - Horizontal integration
   - Vertical integration
   - Diversification
   - Intensification

5. **A more detailed scheme uses the categories-**

   - Prospector
   - Analyser
   - Defender
   - Reactor

- Marketing warfare strategies - This scheme draws parallels between marketing strategies and military strategies.

Strategic Models

Marketing participants often employ strategic models and tools to analyse marketing decisions. When beginning a strategic analyse, the 3Cs can be employed to get a broad understanding of the strategic environment. An Ansoff Matrix is also often used to convey an organisation's strategic positioning of their marketing mix. The 4Ps can / then be utilised to form a marketing plan to pursue a defined C strategy.

Marketing in Practice

The Consumer-Centric Business

There are many companies especially those in the Consumer Package Goods (CPG) mart that adopt the theory of running their business centred on Consumer, Shopper & Retailer needs. Their Marketing departments spend quality time looking for "Growth Opportunities" in their categories by identifying relevant insights (both mindsets and behaviours) on their target Consumers, Shoppers and retail partners. These Growth Opportunities emerge- from changes in market trends, segment dynamics changing and also internal brand or operational business challenges. The Marketing team can then prioritise these Growth Opportunities and begin to develop strategies to exploit the opportunities that could include new or adapted products, services as well as changes to the 7Ps.

Real-life marketing primarily revolves around the application of a great deal of common-sense; dealing with a limited number of factors, in an environment of imperfect information and limited resources complicated by uncertainty and tight timescales. Use of classical marketing techniques, in these circumstances, is inevitably partial and uneven.

Thus, for example, many new products will emerge from irrational processes and the rational development process may be used (if at all) to screen out the worst non-runners. The design of the advertising, and the packaging, will be the output of the creative minds employed; which management will then screen, often by 'gut-reaction', to ensure that it is reasonable.

For most of their time, marketing managers use intuition and experience to analyse and handle the complex, and unique, situations being faced; without easy reference to theory. This will often be 'flying by the seat of the pants', or 'gut-reaction'; where the overall strategy, coupled with the knowledge of the customer which has been absorbed almost by a process of osmosis, will determine the quality of the marketing employed. This, almost instinctive management, is what is sometimes called 'coarse marketing'; to distinguish it from the refined, aesthetically pleasing, form favoured by the theorists.

Ten Categories of Marketing Strategy

The following strategies work. Here they are:

Networking

1. Basics:

   Go "out there" and start hobnobbing or schmoozing with other people in your field. Start "talking up" your product or service. Networking can involve a number of strategies: going to trade shows, speaking at seminars, participating in discussion boards or e-mail discussion lists, going to local chamber of commerce or other places where business people gather. Networking is socialising.

2. Skills:

   You need to have the ability to talk about your product. You need to believe in your product. You need knowledge of your industry and the ability to talk about it. Being a "people person" helps. If you don't consider yourself a people person, then stick to the discussion lists where you have the opportunity to write - be personable through your writing.

3. Time and Money:

   Networking takes time. You need to stick to it. You'll want to try to network in one form or another at least once a week. Networking shouldn't cost you money (unless you're attending seminars or joining the local chamber of commerce.) Networking is a long-term strategy that every business person should engage in.

Direct Mail Marketing

1. Basics:

   Direct marketing comes in the form of sales letters, brochures and flyers. It is a piece of writing that you will mail out to your prospects.

2. Skills:

   You will need writing skills. If you don't have these skills, you might consider hiring a professional publicist. You will need a list of prospects and their addresses.

3. Time and Money:

   Direct marketing will cost money for the initial campaign. You will need to pay for the printing and the mailing, you may need to pay for the layout and the writing. It is a short-term strategy that should bring you leads or sales immediately.

Media Advertising

1. Basics:

   TV, Radio, Magazine and Newspaper ads are all traditional forms of advertising that are used to raise brand awareness. The Yellow Pages are a good choice for long-term advertising of a service that people may need only once in a while.

2. Skills:

   Generally, the place that you choose to advertise will have people available to help you create a good ad campaign.

3. Time and Money:

   This can be an expensive strategy. It is generally a long-term strategy that is used to build brand awareness over a period of time.

Cheap Offline Advertising

1. Basics:

   Classified Advertising, business cards, flyers, promotional items with your business name on them (buttons, hats, pencils).

2. Skills:

   You will need the ability to write short ads.

3. Time and Money:

   This is generally a long-term strategy that creates brand awareness. It is less expensive than Traditional Advertising, however, it has less reach, if you are doing classified ads, it's a short-term strategy that should bring immediate benefits.

Training Programmes

1. Basics:

   A training programme might be set up in several ways:

- online training - you set up the course online.
- training at "their" place of business - you would travel to a company and teach your course.
- training at "your" place of business - you would set up the meeting place and find people to attend. You might develop a training programme to increase awareness of your products. MicroSoft.com makes good use of this strategy.

2. Skills:

   You'll need the ability to teach (or to hire a teacher). You will need to make arrangements for a place to teach.

3. Time and Money:

   This strategy could be time intensive. You will have to set up the course and find the time to teach it. I recommend that you start out online and branch out from there. See if you have the knack for setting up a course syllabus and writing out all of the information you wish to convey. If you can do that, then you may want to take your course "on the road."

Become known as an Expert

1. Basics:

   In order to become an expert, you will need to give out advice. Advice can come in many forms: seminars, training, discussion boards, articles, books, e-books, a website, and/or an e-zine. Generally, you will start out by giving free advice, by getting out there and getting your name recognised. When you get a little notoriety you can start publishing and charging for your advice.

2. Skills:

   In order to become an expert you are going to need skills in at least one of the following areas: writing and/or public speaking.

3. Time and Money:

   Initially, this strategy will take time and lots of it. Eventually, if you decide to publish, you might consider self-publishing. Websites, e-books and e-zines are relatively inexpensive if you do all the dirty work yourself, again it's time consuming. Publishing books will get a little more expensive, but still reasonable considering what some of the other marketing strategies might cost.

Direct Personal Selling

1. Basics:

   Telephone sales and door-to-door sales fall into this category. Also, if you have a brick-and-mortar store, you will also engage in direct sales.

2. Skills:

   Once again, being personable is a needed skill. If you are making cold calls, take the time to write down what you want to say before getting on the phone or going door-to-door. Knowing about your product and believing in your product will help you get the sale. Having sales materials, like a brochure, a flyer and business cards will help you make the sale, especially if your prospects don't have time for you. Offer to mail a brochure or leave a flyer with them.

3. Time and Money:

   This should cost you very little. However it will take up your time. It is a short-term strategy that will lead to immediate sales and possible sales in the long-term.

Publicity and Press Releases

1. Basics:

   Getting the media to recognise you is one of the most influential ways to get people to buy. You immediately gain credibility if the media picks you up. You will need press releases and possibly a press kit or media kit.

2. Skills:

   You will need to learn how to write and distribute your press releases or press kit. You may need to hire a professional publicist.

3. Time and Money:

   This is a risky proposition if you do it yourself: you may end up doing a lot of work and never getting picked up by the press. It can be an expensive proposition if you hire someone else to do it for you. It is both a short-term strategy (you may get immediate sales following any publicity) and a long-term strategy that builds awareness of your business or your product.

Website

1. Basics:

   A website can work in many ways for your business. If it is professional, it will lend credibility, it may give you direct sales or sales leads, it can build awareness of your business.

2. Skills:

   You will either need to learn how to build a site yourself or you can hire a professional developer.

3. Time and Money:

   To start out, a website does not have to be large and complicated. It will either take you time to develop or it will take you money to have someone else create it for you. A website is a long term strategy that you must continually work on and maintain. If used properly, it will create awareness over the long term.

Internet Advertising

1. Basics:

   Search Engines, Online Directories, Banner ads, e-zine ads, e-mail, and your website are all ways to advertise on the Internet.

2. Skills:

   You will need many skills if you plan to do this on your own. You will need to learn how to get ranks in the search engines and online directories, you will need the ability to write ads and/or create banners. If you do not have the time to invest to learn about Internet advertising, you may wish to hire someone to enact this strategy.

3. Time and Money:

   Generally, Internet advertising is one of the less expensive ways to advertise, however, it might take 1 to 6 months to develop a good Internet advertising campaign and to start seeing some result. It is a great way to brand and will also result in direct sales.

❑❑❑

6
Managing and Planning Financial Resources

Managing Financial Resources addresses the complicated issues of financial planning and control. These include performance measures and cost analysis, methods of improving profitability and techniques of financial monitoring and control. It is about getting the most from the resources you have available. It involves implementing resource management procedures and controls and can include managing costs and maximising opportunities.

Ideas and intentions can often outweigh the availability of resources within an organisation. Reviewing your "wish list" against financial and strategic plans will enable you to:

- identify what financial resources are available now and required in the future
- prioritise these resources against objectives and goals
- implement evaluation procedures to ensure resources are maximised
- plan for potential changes that may lay ahead; e.g. change of staff, access to funding, beneficiary need, organisational growth

This process will ensure that strategic goals and budgets are realistic and achievable whilst maintaining some flexibility. As with any process, this should involve a range of people in your organisation.

Just as there are several organisational models for delivering extension services to the public, there are a number of ways to finance those services and to keep track of the money. Sound financial management may be fundamental to success. Poor financial management, on the other hand, often accompanies and contributes to failure.

This topic focuses its attention on principles related to money matters. These concepts as appropriate to situations they face in their own organisations and in accordance with the rules and customs of their own countries. Because people are more readily inclined to apply ideas that deal with practical concerns, this discussion will be organised around practical problems. It will also address some of the major methods found to be most successful in resolving those problems.

The major financial concerns of an extension organisation can be described rather simply:

- Extension organisations have too few financial resources, given the nature and size of their missions.
- Managers and other staff members do not know and apparently cannot find out how many resources are available for use in dealing with a particular problem or programme activity.
- They do not know the costs of carrying out various activities or whether a particular approach is a cost-effective way to deliver programming.
- Money may be committed almost totally to salaries, leaving little to cover operating costs.
- Financial allocation decisions are made by people who are not in a position to know best how the money should be spent.

- Little is known about whether work is being carried out efficiently or what has been the impact of organisation programmes.
- Financial resources are wasted.
- Resources are misappropriated.

Most of what can go wrong in an extension organisation when it comes to money is covered by one or more of the above problems. Managers may be inclined to say that their problems would be solved if they just had more money to work with. And having more money to use is certainly better than having too little. But more money may not always result in greater impact if the money is not well managed.

There may be little connection between quality of programme delivery and an organisation's system for managing money. A specialist's message getting through to a farmer does not totally depend on how much money is spent on the process. However, organisations that are effective tend to know how their money is being spent. A case can easily be made that sound financial management is the first step toward quality programming.

Obtaining Financial Resources

There is an almost universal reaction of managers when it comes to money, namely, they do not have enough of it. They need and want more.

Leaders are responsible for acquiring and maintaining resources for their organisation. These efforts tend to be more successful when requests deal with issues of high national priority and when an explanation is provided as to how the additional resources will be used.

Extension organisations are supported financially from a variety of sources. Publically funded organisations receive support from:

- Public appropriations
- Contracts with other agencies, donors, or both
- Loans
- Gifts
- Income from sales
- User fees

Private extension organisations are financed by:

- Endowment income
- Private investment
- Income-producing activities
- The same sources as public extension organisations

Depending on custom and regulations, extension organisations may receive support from any combination of the above. Currently, there is interest in some countries in "privatising" some functions - that is, shifting certain responsibilities (and the costs associated with them) to privately funded enterprises (NGOs) or directly to users.

But whether the extension effort is private or public, it is not uncommon for financial support to be provided from more than one source. Obviously, the more sources of funding, the more complicated administration is, because most funding sources have their own expectations of outcomes, reporting requirements, and timetables.

Despite administrative complexity, managers often find that having more than one source of funding is advantageous. Several sources provide a hedge against adverse treatment by a single funding partner or source. Special funding sources often help the organisation to focus on emerging, high priority concerns or to test new approaches. A practical goal might be to have a resource commitment from the principal funding partner (the most dependable source of continuing funding) that will maintain the "core" or basic structure of the organisation (e.g., selected staff salaries and other expenses). Support for whatever is beyond the core might then come from the so-called softer resources or some combination of funding sources as described previously. Temporary resources permit experimentation and the carrying out of special projects.

No single ideal ratio of core to total support can be applied everywhere. This is partly because organizations will define what is part of the core and what is left for special or temporary support differently. As a general rule, managers might reasonably seek something like an 80-20 split (core to soft resources).

Keeping Track of Financial Resources

The function of management is to plan, organise, staff, lead, and control. Every one of these functions is influenced to a great degree by how much money there is. Managers and programme staff simply cannot carry out their assigned responsibilities effectively without understanding their financial constraints.

Leaders of extension organisations are accountable for the financial resources assigned. It is incumbent upon them to establish workable systems that will enable staff members to know how many resources they have to carry out their work.

Managers need to have some means for knowing what is happening with respect to their financial resources if they are to make informed management decisions. The notion that leaders of extension organisations are accountable to funding partners is one of the reasons managers need to keep track of how money is spent. The organisation will be expected to report how much money there was, how much was spent, what it was spent for, and how much is left.

This responsibility is carried out by installing and managing a financial accounting system. That system may well be automated at some point, but a manual system will serve most needs at the outset. But regardless of how reports are produced and records maintained, they should be accurate and produced in a timely fashion so that staff can base their decisions on good information. A number of acceptable computer software programmes are available to meet this accounting need. It is generally unnecessary for most organisations to spend time and resources designing and implementing a unique system.

Predicting Organisational Costs

Resources to be committed to any activity are always finite. An extension organisation's need for money and the benefits that accrue from that expenditure compete in theory for resources against all other potential uses.

Budgeting the use of resources to particular purposes and for specific accounting periods is an essential part of the planning and managing processes. This process combined with cost accounting makes it possible to make decisions based on expected costs and returns.

Governments are expected to provide essential services and to use resources for the betterment of citizens. Other funding sources seek to maximise benefits in accordance with their particular goals. And no matter how well endowed the funding sources are, there are always limits to how much they can provide. Budgeting is the technique used by organisations to help determine how many resources will be needed and how they will be used. The budget also is used to help manage the rate of expenditures as the year progresses.

Budgets are typically subdivided into categories that have meaning in the local situation and that help managers and potential funders to understand how money is to be spent. Budget information when compared with actual expenses enables managers and programme staff to stay within assigned allocation levels as they accomplish programme goals.

Maintaining a Balance in How Resources are to be Used?

Some extension organisations simply do not have enough resources to cover normal operating costs. This may be a result of previous decisions that had the effect of protecting staff salaries and staff size at the expense of allocations for operating costs. Or it may be that salary support is provided by a central authority and is not even a part of the organisation's budget. In this situation, when budgets are cut (with little or no change in staff size), it merely means that staff members have fewer resources to use to carry out their work. Or it may be that funds have been provided, but that increases have not kept pace with inflation. The result is that too few resources are available to carry out the work of the organisation. In some organisations, almost no resources exist to cover travel, publications, or any of a wide variety of other possible operating costs.

Managers should seek to align resources in ways that make it possible to accomplish organisational objectives. This usually suggests the need to maintain an appropriate balance between salaries and operating expenses.

It does little good to have a large staff if resources are too limited to provide that staff with the means to get something accomplished. Managers might logically address this problem by reducing the number of positions and increasing expense allocations, thus changing the ratio between salaries and operating expense items. However, such a move might make it necessary to change the way programmes are delivered.

For example, staff may be too few in number to permit visits to individual farmers. If farmers are to be reached in this situation, it may be necessary to bring them together in groups. Or the result may be that only a small number of individual farmers can be reached. In some countries, national regulations do not make it easy to exchange personnel resources for money to use for operating costs, or vice versa, or even to avoid unfunded programme responsibilities. In those situations especially, managers might seek help from alternative funding sources. However, if the problem can be resolved simply by reallocation, that is often the most straight forward approach. Establishing user fees and charging for publications are other ways to obtain additional resources when reallocations between salaries and expenses are not possible. The problem with the latter approaches is that targeted audiences may not have resources to pay user fees or to buy publications. Consequently, these approaches can have negative effects on programme impact.

There is probably no single "best" ratio to maintain between salaries and expense resources. The percentage of total resources spent on salaries might vary with the mixture of staff members (e.g., the number of village workers or paraprofessionals and the number of subject-matter specialists). The amount of operating resources required to carry out the mission will be affected by geography, size of country, and method of programme delivery. However, as a general guide, if salary costs require more than 75 to 80 per cent of total resources, this is a fairly good indication that operating funds may be beginning to limit success.

Decentralising the Decision-making Process

The purpose of an extension organisation is to deliver practical problem-solving educational programmes and to carry out various other designated activities. These activities tend to be very location specific. Yet the tendency is to structure extension organisations according to a "command" or top-down decision-making model. However, this approach has been found wanting time and again. In fact, the opposite condition appears to yield the best results when it comes to actually carrying out programmes. It appears that decentralised decision making is almost essential if an organisation is to be responsive to the people being served. In short, central staff should limit their decision making to determining financial commitments to programme areas and leave decisions regarding how money is spent in support of programmes to others closer to the scene.

The determination of how money is to be spent may best be made by those who are directly carrying out activities that serve intended clientele.

Who better than the people delivering programmes know what is needed? And who would know better how to spend an additional resource (were it to be available) to achieve greater benefit? Research suggests that the answer to these questions is that teams of programme leaders, specialists, and others in direct contact with clientele are in better positions than central staffs are to make informed programme decisions and to spend money wisely.

If this kind of decentralised decision making is to be accomplished, organisational resources will have to be subdivided among programme units. And programme leaders and others will need to be given authority and responsibility to make decisions about how money is to be spent. If this is simply not possible under existing rules, then such decisions should be made by staff members who are as close to the programme level as is possible.

Decisions regarding centrally managed financial reserves should be made so that needs with the highest priority can be addressed. And of course, it is a wise practice to maintain a reserve fund centrally to deal with emerging and unforeseen events.

Using Information to Improve Efficiency

There has been much discussion in the literature about whether extension organisations are appropriate vehicles to use to bring about agricultural development, to avoid rapid urbanisation, and even what kinds of activities to include under the extension rubric. A lot of research has been conducted that is designed to determine the "outcomes" from extension education. A considerable body of research deals with these issues. But managers cannot get by leaving those issues entirely to research institutions. They are expected by stakeholders to efficiently manage resources assigned to them.

Efficiency is a relative measure. Efficiency can be implied by sets of physical data compared over time or among categories (e.g., number of pages produced per editor, this time period compared with an earlier time period).

Efficiency can also measured in monetary terms (e.g., cost of delivering a particular message per 100 users compared with another delivery method or another time period).

Organisations typically create some kind of feedback mechanism to collect needed data from staff and others when they want to take measurements of efficiency. Many organisations assign staff and other resources to coordinate the task of collecting the necessary information. Often, data collection and analysis are a full-time responsibility of a programme monitoring unit or a management information system (MIS) unit.

The monitoring unit will need to obtain appropriate data from the organisation's financial information system to determine costs of various undertakings and to compute input-output ratios. These cost estimates or ratios, when compared over time and between different approaches, help staff to know which methods or approaches are more efficient.

It is possible to collect almost unlimited amounts of data about programme activities. Management's responsibility is to select from a large potential array what is import enough to collect (as well as how often) and how best to collect and analyse it. Organisations should avoid collecting more data than they can effectively use, because this needlessly wastes staff time and resources.

Using Information to Increase Effectiveness

While it is important for organisations to efficiently carry out their missions, they also need to be concerned about effectiveness. An organisation is said to be effective if it accomplishes its stated objectives. Ideally, an organisation should be both effective and cost efficient.

Effectiveness is a measure of programme impact as compared with the intended goals. To measure effectiveness, organisations must collect programme impact data. An organisation that is both effective and cost efficient is achieving its goals, and the benefits obtained are greater than the costs involved.

To determine whether an organisation is effective, it is necessary to look at programme impact. To obtain programme impact measurements, organisations either use the services of external specialists (to avoid the appearance or the reality of bias), or they create a capability within their organisation to measure programme impacts.

But whether external or internal resources are used, the effort needs to be conducted professionally and in an unbiased fashion.

The programme impact unit or external service will need to measure programme impact in context - that is to say, a low-budget undertaking with a very limited goal can be said to have been effectively carried out if the stated goal was achieved.

Any number of programme impact studies can be conducted. But they cost money and staff time. The management responsibility is to determine which outcomes are important enough to measure at a particular point in time, to ensure that efforts to measure those outputs are properly carried out and analysed, and then to use the information in decision making. The first such use should be directed at making changes that will cause future programme efforts to be more successful.

Those who manage or who provide resources to extension organisations are interested in two kinds of measurements - those that indicate the organisation is productive and efficient and those that help to determine if the organisation is effective. The former tend to be measurements of inputs and outputs, and the latter tend to be project impacts.

Wasting Resources

Waste can be found in all kinds of organisations: public and private, profit and non-profit. A commonly held view is that public organisations tend to "waste" more resources the other kinds do. This view holds that private organisations are motivated by profits, and consequently they avoid waste to a greater extent than "non-profits." Alternatively, public organisations often are required to adhere to a higher standard of accountability. Consequently, the profit or non-profit question may not be the major determining factor. But whether public or private, profit or non-profit, waste increases costs and decreases benefits.

Resources can be wasted if decisions are poor or are not made in a timely fashion. They are wasted if they are not used to best advantage (e.g., if more is bought than is needed or if the purchase price was not competitive).

Organisations can avoid waste by creating appropriate policies. Those policies then need to be translated into procedures designed to achieve policy goals. Finally, managers need to administer the procedures fairly and consistently, and staff members affected by the procedures need to cooperate in the effort.

Organisations need something more than high-sounding platitudes along the line of "waste not, want not." Policies and operating procedures need to be couched in terms of real-world situations faced by the organisation. For example, organisations need to establish policies and procedures that determine how purchases are to be made (including when and by whom) and how sales, if any, are to be handled (including what happens to the money). It should be clear to staff members what their authorities and with respect to spending money. And those staff members who are not allowed to spend the organisation's money need to know who they should turn to for a decision. To the extent there is confusion, there is likely to be waste.

Misappropriating Resources

Organisational resources sometimes are used by staff members or others for personal gain. Resources may simply be stolen. Misappropriation of resources negatively affects an organisation's reputation, and its ability to carry out its mission. Costs are increased, and thus its ability to accomplish its mission and to attract additional resources is jeopardized. To protect against these eventualities, organisations should institute and administer policies and procedures designed to discourage and prevent these behaviour. There should be appropriate supervision and a periodic auditing of financial records and procedures.

Organisational resources should be used to further organisational goals. Staff members should not be permitted to use their positions for personal gain.

The problem of misappropriation of organisational resources appears to be widespread. It is found in both developed and developing countries. It may entail pilfering supplies or taking money. It may involve payments to individual staff members who require such payments before they will render services or for special treatment.

To avoid waste, loss of productivity, negative impacts on staff morale, and loss of confidence by clients being served, organisations need to take steps to avoid losses from misappropriation. They should administer procedures fairly, and then act in ways appropriate to regulation and law.

Financial Planning

Planning is one of the key to success of any undertaking, and nowhere is it more important than in business. Every sturdy dealing with business failures uncovers the basic problem, whether it is called undercapitalisation, poor location, or simply a lack of managerial skills. All these problems have their roots in planning. For planning to be successful, it must be founded in a root philosophy or conceptual framework that provides a basis for analysis, execution, and evaluation.

Financial planning is the task of determining how a business will afford to achieve its strategic goals and objectives. Usually, a company creates a Financial Plan immediately after the vision and objectives have been set. The Financial Plan describes each of the activities, resources, equipment and materials that are needed to achieve these objectives, as well as the timeframes involved.

The Financial Planning activity involves the following tasks:

- Assess the business environment
- Confirm the business vision and objectives
- Identify the types of resources needed to achieve these objectives
- Quantify the amount of resource (labour equipment, materials)
- Calculate the total cost of each type of resource
- Summarise the costs to create a budget
- Identify any risks and issues with the budget set

Performing Financial Planning is critical to the success of any organisation. It provides the Business Plan with rigour, by confirming that the objectives set are achievable from a financial point of view. It also helps the CEO to set financial targets for the organisation, and reward staff for meeting objectives within the budget set.

A financial plan consists of sets of financial statements that forecast the resource implications of making business decisions. For example, a company that is deciding to expand e.g. by buying and fitting out a new factory will create a financial plan which considers the resources required and the financial performance that will justify their use. You can see from this statement that the financial plan will need to take into account sources of finance, costs of finance, costs of developing the project, as well as the revenues and likely profits to justify the expansion programme.

Planning models may consist of thousands of calculations. Typically these plans will be constructed with the aid of forecasting models and spreadsheets that can calculate and recalculate figures such as profit, cash flows and balance sheets simply by changing the assumptions. For example, the business may want to do one set of calculations for low, medium, and high demand figures for its products.

Long and Short Term Plans

Financial plans are typically made out for a given time period, e.g. one, three or five years. The length of the time considered depends on the importance of projecting into the future and the reliability of estimates the further we consider the future.

Long-term plans are created for major strategic decisions made by a business such as:

- take over and merger activity

- expansion of capacity
- development of new products
- overseas expansion.

In addition financial planning will be carried out for shorter time spans. For example, annual budgets will be created which can be analysed by month and by cost centre.

Short term financial plans then provide targets for junior and middle management, and a measure against which actual performance can be monitored and controlled. In addition it is normal practice for a business to prepare a three- or five- year plan in less detail, which is updated annually.

A budget is a short term financial plan. It is sometimes referred to as a plan expressed in money - but it is more accurately described as a plan involving numbers.

A cost centre is defined by CIMA as 'a production or service location, function, activity or item of equipment whose costs may be attributed to cost units'.

❑❑❑

7
Maintain Workplace Relationships

The importance of having relationships in the workplace today's competitive workplace is often filled with noisy disputes and legal actions, which sap the precious resources of time and capital from an organisation. Since our professional connections often are forced by time and circumstance our social connections as well, it is important for organisations to facilitate dynamic relationships in the workplace. The organisations that promote an environment where employees and management develop good working relationships will be the winners.

Many of the same dynamics and difficulties exist for relationships in the workplace as do for those outside the workplace. One of the greatest losses to an organisation having no real, satisfying relationships in the workplace. Successful organisations are the ones that create an environment that encourages people to create relationships, which encourages people to be their creative, whole selves. Having a good working relationship with a coworker means trust, and trust assumes that the other person is going to come through for you. Its management's job to see that everyone's goal is to come through for one another.

In many years of consulting with organisations of all sizes and types, relationships turning disastrous in the workplace

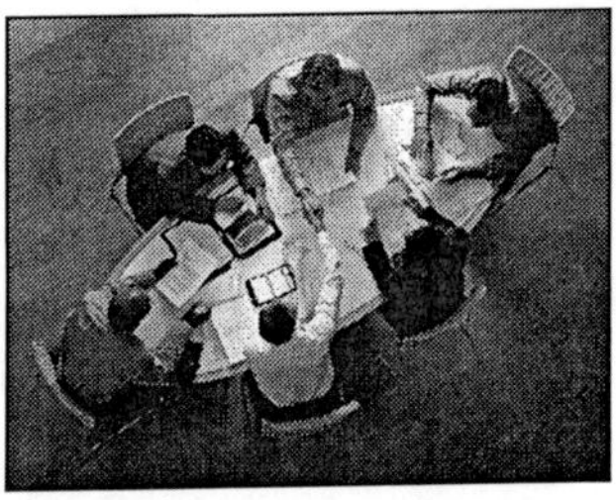

are all premised on a competitive environment. That must change if your organisation is going to be successful. The workplace should be about working together, about partnership. There are very few situations in which an organisation moves forward when one employee wins by making sure another one loses. If an employee knows something of value that could help everyone, but doesn't share that information because of competition, everyone loses.

The decision to explore or eschew good working relationships should not be put solely on the shoulders of each individual employee. Much of the responsibility falls on management, which must strive to make the workplace one in which supportive, non-competitive relationships can flourish. Employees should never be pitted against one another. They should never be made to feel unworthy or left out. The emphasis should be on cohesion and the common good, with group goals and teamwork focus. While it is management's duty to facilitate dynamic relationships in the workplace, the individual employee still has responsibilities as well. Whether working in an environment in which competition is encouraged or defused, there are certain, specific steps an individual can take to make sure good working relationships survive at work:

- Talk about things that are upsetting you in your work relationship.
- Don't avoid the real issues.
- Listen to each other's point of view.
- Don't try to convince the other person that you are right and he or she is wrong.
- Don't take either/ or, this, you/ me positions.

- Assume that maintaining a good working relationship is as important as, if not more important than, anything happening at work.

If managers and their employees all conscientiously attempt to keep the work environment clear of competition, then many potentially damaging relationship complications and crises will be more easily handled, doing much less ultimate harm to all those involved than they might otherwise do.

Quality relationships are what produce quality products and services. Real productivity begins with employees who are nourished by caring, encouraging coworkers and supervisors. It's an atmosphere where personal creativity can really flourish. While caring about an employee's emotional well-being and the healthiness of his or her relationships may not be part of anyone's? Official? Job description, it is a genuine key to creating quality products and services.

It's incumbent upon senior management in particular to wholeheartedly support personal growth in individuals further down the employment ladder; otherwise, an environment will persist in which growth cannot and will not take place. However, the responsibility to create a supportive environment involves all employees. Just as a CEO can be caring and encouraging, so too can an hourly employee. When it comes to understanding emotions and relationships, there are no status levels.

The workplace can often be a very angry place, and the relationships there can be irreparably harmed by anger and mistrust. In fact when it comes to relationships among colleagues anger and mistrust often arise out of issues in the work relationship. A successful organisation is one that faces these issues head-on, that discusses them openly and encourages good working relationships, caring, and trust.

At the heart of it all is communication. The secret to healing in the workplace is to get people talking, a process not nearly as elementary as it might sound. Employees do not always want to talk about work. Often, in groups of their colleagues, they talk about themselves, who they are, what they dream about, and, what they resent and fear. They discuss things friends usually talk about, not people who happen to share the same work space. When people reveal themselves to coworkers, when they openly discuss their feelings with honesty and compassion, when they are truly understood as individuals, the stage is set for meaningful workplace relationships between people who are real, and not just figures hurrying down a hall or across a plant floor. This, in turn, feeds and facilitates the more impersonal, yet worthy and essential goals of an organisation: quality, productivity, and the bottom line.

For the most part management doesn't have to do anything extraordinary for a relationship-supportive environment to exist. If an organisation offers fair compensation, has an equitable system of promotion in place, and rewards work done on its merit, the relationships in the workplace will take care of themselves. You can't arrange people to get along with one another. That is like parents trying to select or match up their children. It can't be done. These things, these relationships just happen. Business is 90 percent relationships. You can't do business without them. But there must be a delicate balance between relationships and friendships. For example, managers should know not to become great drinking buddies with the people they supervise. Just as they should also know not to become close friends with the chairman.

On the other hand, don't be aloof. Maintain a positive relationship that doesn't impose on you, the other person, or the work to be done. These are common sense things managers learn as they mature. Cultivating relationships in the workplace ultimately comes down to the individual employees. An organisation can and should try to facilitate relationships in the workplace but it comes down to individual styles or individual needs as human beings. Because of the type of organisation and the diversity of the workplace it will vary from workplace to workplace, manager to manager, and friend to friend.

The quality of the relationship between officials and competitors makes an important contribution to the success of competition, both for competitors and spectators. Officials need to be able to establish and maintain their authority over competition whilst gaining the respect and co-operation of competitors. Often officials need to liaise with competitors' representatives-such as coaches, physios and team managers-as well in order to deal with objections and queries, and it is important that there is a similar level of respect and co-operation. Conflicts will sometimes occur with or between competitors and the official needs to be able to deal with these conflicts smoothly and effectively whilst maintaining their authority.

But as we move further into the 21st Century, it may well turn out that the success of an organisation pivots on its ability to tap into something very basic, something as old and entrenched as mankind itself: the need to establish relationships, to connect with someone else.

The workplace relationships advantage:

- Enhance retention of key talent.
- Develop the courage to take meaningful risks on your own behalf.
- Understand the difference between leading people and renting them.
- Cultivate the best of smallness within large organisations.

Maintain Professional Relationships with Your Competitors

Sometimes business owners think about competition as the "big, bad wolf" that is only after their customers and is eroding their profit margins.

In reality, the same people you are in competition with can turn out to be one of your most valuable assets. How do you ask? Simple. By partnering with competitors, small business owners can develop the necessary network to function like a larger company. They can help business owners provide extended services, deal with emergencies, and tap into a referral market that can be lucrative.

While every business would like to provide every service to their customers, the reality is much different. Often, small business owners have to turn away customers because of the complexity of the services requested.

If small business owners have a professional relationship with their competitors, they will be able to pool those resources together to carry out the project. Take, for example, event planners. They have to piece together large events that require multiple moving parts. In order to accomplish this, they might need to turn to their competitors for linens, tables, lighting fixtures or other materials.

In addition, a tightly knit strategic alliance with competitors can yield benefits in the times of crisis. Over the years, I have seen and heard about business owners pulling resources together to help their competitors after a fire or a natural disaster. Business owners realise competitors are people too, and there is nothing more rewarding than extending a helping hand during someone's time of need.

While resources and helping hands are great benefits of strong alliances with competitors, ultimately business owners are in business to make money. Strategic alliances can also help. Take, for example, the limousine driver who is overbooked. To please his customers, the driver will refer them to another company that can handle their request for service.

The first companies that he will refer these customers to will be those he has professional relationships with, or those that have referred customers to him in the past.

To business owners, competitors can be an everyday burden, but they can also be a lifeline in times of need. Developing and maintaining those relationships can be a worthwhile venture to companies big and small.

These relationships can provide additional resources, help deal with emergencies, and provide additional referrals.

Not every competitor is a good business partner, but it does not hurt to have existing relationships with as many of them as possible. The main things to remember when partnering with competitors is to always keep your most valued customers at home, never reveal too many company secrets, and try to reciprocate when it is appropriate.

Maintain Business Relationship with Your Competitors

As a business, your competitors are just that competitors. However, the way you treat your competitors may affect how your customers and the media perceive your business, your ethics, and your friendliness. For those reasons, and more, it's important that you carefully consider how you act with your competitors. It is possible to have a good relationship with competing businesses while limiting the impact they will have on your business success. When customers see you treating your competitors fairly, they will have more respect for you. Here are some ways to maintain good business relationship with your competitors:

1. **Congratulate their success**

   When a competing business does something well, you should be prepared to say so. If for example, a competing business has managed to gain greater traction than you, then you should point out that they have done really well, and are a good business, while also pointing out the advantages your business is able to offer that your competitors cannot. This is a good demonstration of the strong beliefs you have for your business, and will certainly leave a positive impression. At the same time look at ways of overtaking your competitor in all

2. **Recommend business their way**

   If you and your competitors are able to cater for different categories of customers, then why not recommend them when you can't offer the required service to a certain customer? This will make you look good in both your customers and competitors eyes, and they might also be able to do the same for you in return. In the end, both of you will hopefully end up with more business as a result.

3. **Sales and marketing strategies**

   When it comes to sales and marketing, it can be tempting to point out the negative aspects of your competitors. And, in some cases, it may be an essential part of closing the sale. However, rather than criticising your competitor, why not mention both positive and negative points of their service? Such as: "Yes, you are correct, Company A is able to offer lower pricing than we can. For customers that are more price sensitive, and that 100% up-time isn't essential, they can be a great solution. We cater for more IT-dependent organisations and employ 3 times as many engineers per customer. Company A also use an overseas call-centre, which is a great way to keep costs down, and provide a more efficient service, but we prefer to assign each customer a dedicated account manager to provide better service."

However, on some occasions your competitors may not provide a good service. In this case, you should be as polite and tactful about your competitors as possible. Rather than voicing your own opinions, you should cite sources, such as articles and media coverage that make your point for you. After pointing out any negative issues, you might also wish to explain how your company responds to the same problems. This will show a certain level of objectivity on your part and will demonstrate that your business has strong ethics and is willing to appreciate your competitors' problems.

4. **Don't bite**

   When a competitor speaks negatively about your business, it can be hard to know what to do. Especially when you want to ensure your business appears to be friendly and considerate of others. Although it's important to respond to any issues in an articulate way, you should avoid getting involved in any tit-for-tat. This will help your business stand out from the crowd.

Target Competitors

Winning in business usually means doing a few things very well indeed: developing progressively deeper customer relationships, targeting defined competitors and creating competitively superior customer value. Many companies choose to focus on the first issue, believing that customer-focused marketing creates more shareholder value than beating competitors. But if competitors are looking for business in the same places as you and if some have secured the relationships you also want, you may need to target them. Seek to transfer share of customer to your firm, to ensure that you have a larger share of the customer's future than they do, and even to transfer accounts where they presently have strong relationships. This requires that you not only understand the quality of the relationships your company enjoys with its customers, but also the quality of the relationships your competitors have in your priority accounts and prospects. This can lead to a more complete assessment of specific competitors. This is competitor targeting. Which competitors represent an opportunity for your firm? Which must you overcome to win? Is beating defined competitors part of all the management decisions your firm makes? For example, when recruiting a new Vice President, do you ask if the prospect is better than the person in place in the competitor is? When deciding on a new computer system, do you similarly ask if this is better than competitors' and better able to develop the customer relationships you seek? What we are arguing for here, is an integration of competitive intelligence and customer relationship assessments, leading to competitive advantage over defined losers so that you can win.

In turn, these assessments need to be integrated with your strategic planning processes. This is important ensure that any assessment of customer relationships and competitors precedes the strategic planning process and integrates with it. This will help ensure that your plans are fact-based and provide a realistic basis to grow. Also ensure that your plans benefit from an assessment of the actions competitors could take and how you, in turn, would respond to their actions. These contingent responses should be a part of your planning process, too. Thinking this through, some companies find they need to revisit their entire strategic planning processes and ensure that their thinking and processes have the potential for beating competitors and accelerating business performance.

Some competitors may be cold, hostile and unwilling to share information, but others in your field may be more than willing to share tips and tricks of the trade. In fact, if there's a work overload, some competitors will refer customers to one another.

There are several ways to connect with your competitors. One way is to attend local chapter meetings of trade associations for your industry. (This also can be a good way to meet business prospects; corporate workers in a position to hire independent contractors often attend such meetings.)

Another way is to become active in local or regional business groups that are not industry-specific. Chambers of Commerce, Toastmasters, Lions Club and regional business associations are examples. If your product or service is sold to local businesses, you are very likely to meet competitors (as well as sales prospects) at such meetings.

If networking with local competitors doesn't suit you, seminars at industry trade shows can be a source for supplier information, tips for operating more efficiently, and possibly competitive information.

❑❑❑

8
Learn From Your Competitors

It seems screamingly obvious, doesn't it? Intensely monitor your competitors to determine what can be learned -- and then, if it makes sense -- appropriate from them. For the most part it's wise and perfectly legal larceny.

So why, in my experience, doesn't it happen nearly enough? The answer is that we often spend a lot of time studying our competitors for weaknesses, but we seldom try to incorporate their strengths--their wisdom and experience--because we think they're stupid.

It's true. We are often victims of our culture of vilification and crude mockery. It's a rare moment when we celebrate our competitors for their boldness of vision, their ability to execute and implement their organisational prowess.

Sure, we look at "best practices," but usually they are outside our industry or category. It's safe to praise those we're not locked in mortal combat with. So even though there's a cautionary adage that reminds us to "never underestimate your enemy."

To add another layer to this, I believe this sin is most often a problem in entrepreneurial businesses. That's because we take our companies so personally, and it's difficult to learn from someone we dislike, worry about, or even fear.

So what's the solution? Step back and assess your competitors through this clarifying lens. It will help focus your efforts in a meaningful and productive fashion, and also provide some valuable corporate introspection as well.

First, take a look back on 2008. What are the five smartest things your three largest competitors did? And don't just ask yourself, ask your senior management team, too.

Send an e-mail as soon as you finish reading this. Ask them to make a complete, full MRI scan of your competitors' efforts: marketing, sales, R&D, the works.

Then examine the results. Were those things you considered and rejected? Were they initiatives you hadn't thought of? What impact did they have on your business and what learning can you derive for next year based on them? What is it about your competitors that created conditions for these business wins?

Which leads us to the next step on the ladder of self-examination? What is it about your competitors organisations that enable them to have any advantage over you in the marketplace? (Be honest: It's a rare and unusual business that has competitors who aren't successful in at least one or two dimensions.)

For example, take the HR side. Do they have better people? Are their compensation policies more lucrative? Is it a better environment for people to work? Are they faster at bringing new products to market? Go through the same exercise about other key functional areas, and then identify the ones that have the highest levels of saliency - and put together a plan to improve your competitive abilities.

Another way to learn about your competition is from a bit of role playing. Put yourself in the shoes of your largest nemesis. What does he (or she) think of you? What is their CIA profile of your personality and behaviour? Can you identify patterns in his strategy based upon his expectation of what your next move is?

In much of the consulting work I've done, I've noted the predictable nature of corporate leadership. CEOs like to repeat what works and are usually afraid to try something that has failed--even if it failed for reasons that are no longer valid, or are correctable.

This is no surprise to canny competitors. So next year, surprise yourself--and them. Employ some of the strategies of the battlefield and the chessboard, rather than last year's conference report.

Take some time away from studying the lessons of the business books and the legendary brand name leaders they celebrate. And spend some time studying the guy who wants to eat your lunch. You might learn something. By taking the time to investigate what has made their businesses work, you'll be able to learn their best methods and improve upon their model. Here are some ways to do your research:

- Shop the competition: Identify them through the phone book, online research, or through word of mouth.
- Analyse their Websites: Search the Internet and read what your competitors say about their own products and services. This also helps you to see how they use the Web for advertising and as a marketing tool.
- Read the local newspaper daily: Find out what special pricing policies, discounts, and incentives they offer. This will give you an idea about their advertising strategy.
- Mingle with competitors: Attending industry seminars and meetings provides opportunities to learn a lot about them in a non-threatening environment.

- Visibility in the community: Find out if your competitors are supporting local charities or community activities. Also look to see if they are exhibiting at trade shows or community business expos.

Competitive information is essential to creating a successful business plan. By conducting this thorough competitive analysis, you will be able to make a successful move into business ownership.

When it comes to strategic marketing, competitors can provide the best insights. Brick-and-mortar marketers have shopped the competition forever. You should, too. Competitive assessment should be conducted as part of the annual business planning process at a minimum. Less formally, it should be done continually.

Determine the Competitive Set

The lynchpin of any competitive assessment is determining the competitive set. Marketers use too restrictive a competitive set to provide sufficient insights. Cast a wide net when developing a list. Include direct competitors, major players in your market (even if they aren't considered a competitor due to size), and firms in the same business as yours who operate in different channels or only in a limited niche. To this list, add the dominant broad-line players in your market. If you're an e-tailer, consider how Amazon and eBay approach your market online and how Wal-Mart or Home Depot approach it offline.

Gather Competitive Insights

Collect information across a wide range of functionality. Consider both the seller and the consumer perspectives. Test and track the consumer experience. Depending on the type of business, this may translate to registering for various newsletters as well as shopping their various services. As you go through each step, consider how efficient and effective the process is. Among the components to track:

1. **Business strategy**

   How does this entity conduct business? What is its business objective? What is its business model?

2. **Markets**

   What markets is it in? How does it segment its customer base?

3. **Offering**

   How does it define its product offering? Include cost and other aspects of the offer. How does it think about its products? Are products and brands categorised, cross-sold, or both? If relevant, assess its suppliers and distributors.

4. **Third-party data**

   Track your ranking within your category as well as relative to your near competitors. Options include Nielsen/NetRatings, comScore, and Hitwise. If your budget's limited, try Alexa and its newer competitors, Quantcast and Site Snapshot.

5. **Website**

   Assess the major components of each website. Are any merchandising components missing? Study how each competitor approaches its site.

6. **Content**

   How is information presented and organised? What content is open and available? What content is used to engage the target market?

7. **Site merchandising**

   What techniques are used to attract visitors? What techniques are used to convert visitors into buyers?

8. **Search functionality**

   Is there search functionality on the site? Research terms competitors use. Monitor keyword buys and placements in search results.

9. **Information gathering**

   How does it collect e-mail addresses? Does it offer information such white papers or catalogues? Are RSS feeds available? Register for these offerings.

10. **Shopping experience**

    Shop the competition where it makes sense, and test different scenarios to see how the consumer's treated. Purchase and return product. Monitor costs, timing, and correspondence.

11. **Distribution channels**

    What distribution channels are available?

12. **Offline presence**

    Check competitors' offline presence, where applicable, and integration with online.

13. **Advertising, press, and buzz**

    Monitor competition in the press, online and off. Assess noise in the marketplace. At a minimum, use Google Alerts, Bloglines, and Technorati. Check other forms of on- and offline advertising and PR.

Three Competitive Analysis Tools

After you've gathered competitive information, it's necessary to organise it. Three techniques to help you gain the most insights from the data:

Develop a Competitive Grid

A grid is useful for organising the data and presenting it in a concise format that highlights differences between competitors. It allows recipients to readily grasp the salient points.

List companies on the vertical axis and attributes on the horizontal. Since there's a lot of information to integrate, break it down into a number of different grids organised category, such as business strategy, website, product and pricing, and offline marketing.

Build a Gap Analysis

As you assess each competitor, note areas of difference for which your firm should have, equivalent functionality. After you've aggregated the information into a competitive grid, seek out other areas where your firm's offering isn't equivalent to its near substitutes.

Compile this list of areas for improvement into a grid that shows the gap on the left and the recommended action to improve your offering on the right. Once you've finished, organise these gaps by major category.

Create a Strengths-Weaknesses-Opportunities-Threats (SWOT) Analysis

A SWOT analysis is a grid that lays out the top competitive issues. Its simplicity is part of its popularity as a management tool. While it may be tempting to place more factors in the strengths and opportunities lists, my preference is for lists that are relatively equal in length. You're usually less aware of your negatives than your positives.

Smart as you are arid as good as your business model is, there's almost always something to learn from competitors. You aren't alone in trying to do a better job. At the very least, you want to know if new threats out there. Often, the best business ideas come from seeing something new or interesting your competitors are doing and adapting it to enhance your product line, offer, target market, distribution, or cost structure.

Who are Your Competitors?

You need to find your competition to learn from them. It could be a teammate, a rival business, or it could be yourself, but the bottom line is that there is someone or something out there that you need to compete with. But how do you find them? Who is considered competition and why?

People and businesses compete for limited resources. We compete for sales, customer's time, or that one promotion, or that one corner office. In short, your competition is anyone who prevents you from getting more of what you want.

You can easily define your competition by looking at your goals. If you want that promotion, your competition is anyone who may receive that promotion over you. If you create video games, your competition is all video game companies or more broadly, any company that demands a person's "extra" time.

But what if you can't find your competitors?

You need to define your business and goals on a broad landscape. It will help you spot potential attackers and growth opportunities. For example, if you specialise in "7 screws, you would not want to compete in the 7 screw" market. You would want to compete in the "we help you build or hang things on the wall" market. If you specialise in Phone games, you need to compete with "we help you waste time on your phone at work" market.

Okay, but how many competitors should you track?

The magic number is all of them. Unfortunately, who has the time for that? So, if you are a small business or corporate executive, I would focus on 3 competitors. If you don't have 3, redefine your business and goals so you have 3. If you have more than 3, redefine your business and goals so you have 3.

You may think 3 is too much or 3 is too little, but it is a very manageable number for a single person. On average, you should spend at least 3 hours per competitor per month and 9 hours isn't too demanding for one person. If you have the resources and time, you should expand your competitor tracking, but if you don't, 3 is a great start.

Things to Learn from Your Competitors

Successful companies know what their competitors are up to at any moment. They use their knowledge of the competition to help develop a strategy for crushing them. How well do you know your competition? Here is something you can learn from your competitors to better prepare your business to compete with them in the online market.

1. **Keywords they are targeting**

   Understanding which keywords your competitors are targeting gives you a clearer idea of how competitive your industry is online. This isn't to say you should directly lift your competitors' keywords, but knowing the phrases they think customers are typing into the search engines is important because it allows you to create a well rounded keyword list. Perform your own keyword research on their key phrases to determine which phrases are worth using.

2. **Keywords they aren't targeting**

   Even more important than the keywords your competition is targeting are the ones they aren't. One easy way to do this is to enter the urls of your competition into the Google Adwords keyword tool. The tool will then suggest additional keywords for those sites to target. Find the most effective keywords that they aren't currently using on their website, and you will be able to make a splash on the SERPs.

3. **Who's linking to them**

   Many website owners say link building is the hardest part of their internet marketing efforts. A good place to start your link building campaign is to study your competitor's inbound links. I prefer using Yahoo as an easy way to look at backlinks. Simply enter linkdomain: www.yourcompetitorssite.com to find info on your competitors backlinks.

4. **Their PPC techniques**

   If you plan on launching a PPC campaign, you can learn a lot from your competition. Search for keywords, and see which competitors are bidding on the PPC terms. You can get a better overall analysis of your competition's PPC strategies by letting an SEQ company handle the work for you.

5. **Their off site efforts**

   What else are your competitors doing besides their main website? Search for their names in Google, and see what comes up. If they have a strong Internet marketing plan, you'll likely find them in social networks, article directories, press release websites, forums, and blogs. Take note of where your competitors are placing their marketing efforts. It will help you come up with a plan for surpassing them.

Things to Learn about Your Competitors Success

Your company is in a precarious position. The marketplace is changing daily. New companies enter the industry. Your competitors are constantly unveiling new products, new services, and/or new marketing strategies. How do you keep up with - or even better, how do you anticipate -- these changes? It may be difficult to find information about future plans of your competitors. However, it sometimes is possible to find information informally, through contacts with their customers, staff or other suppliers. You may be able to find out about new developments in their business or new products that they plan to offer in the future. Here are some tips to know about your competitor business:

1. **Just by virtue of being at the show, your competitors are sharing the following information:**
    - Who they are.
    - What their reputation and image is in the marketplace.
    - Part of their sales and marketing strategy.
2. **Now visit your competitor's booth**

    Before you talk to the booth staff, try to discern the following:
    - Do they pose a threat to my company? Is their booth larger, better designed, more expensive, and filled with substantially more attendees than yours?
    - What is the depth of their product/service offerings?
    - What products and services are they choosing to
    - What features are they emphasising?

    Make note of important differences between your competitors, especially if these disparities create any opportunities in the marketplace that your company could take advantage of.
3. **Be subtle when talking with the booth staff**

    They don't want to give away valuable industry information any more than you do - but you can still learn a lot during the course of a brief conversation, including the following items a general attendee would want to know:

- Product/service features and specifications. Don't get too technical, or you'll scare the booth staff off.
- Most recent product/service introductions.
- Ease of product installation and maintenance.
- Delivery schedule.
- Company and branch locations.
- Quality and service strengths and weaknesses (or what could be improved).
- Pricing strategies: commercial, non-profit, governmental
- Special pricing policies - do they offer: credit, discounts, incentives, consignments
- What is their corporate and business philosophy

4. **Move on to more intrusive questions**

After you have developed a rapport with the booth staff, you can move on to more intrusive questions, including:

- Who are their suppliers? Are they satisfied? Would they consider switching vendors? What are their complaints and unmet needs? What are the key factors in their purchasing decisions?
- Has the company integrated changing industry technology to create cost savings-again, be very general here. If you say "Gee, have you all adopted the new X-7T die cutting laser protocol?" or some other very technical question, they'll know you're not just a random attendee.
- If your competitors have made any important aquisitions over the last year, giving them a competitive advantage.

- Who do they see as the leaders in the industy? You can tell a lot about a company by the firms it tries to emulate.

5. **Learn from your competitors' success**

Some questions are particularly valuable, as they will help you discover the competitor's market share and learn a great deal about their distribution channels. Pay special attention to any markets that your competitors serve that you don't-what can you learn from their success?

- Who are their largest and most important customers?
- Why do customers choose the competitor's products and services?
- What do they consider most valuable about the competitor's products?
- How is their sales staff organised? Would you be dealing with a local, regional, or national sales rep?
- What market efforts, above and beyond trade shows, does the company engage in? Are they equally represented in all areas of the country or are their regional strengths and weaknesses?

Three Easy Ways to Learn about Your Competition

Keeping track of your competitor's activities and progress within the market is an essential part of your market research plan, but many small businesses overlook the work needed to maintain records on the competition, simply due to lack of time and resources. It's a good idea to put even a simple tracking system in place that can help you gauge where your competition is striking next; not only can this help you evaluate your own marketing plans, but can also give you a much better idea of where to set your sights next. Here are just three easy ways to learn about your competition in almost any industry or domain:

1. **Create charts on their products, pricing, and rates**

   This will help you draw a side-by-side comparison on your own products and prices, making it much easier to develop an average price point for future products, and also give you an idea of how similar (or different) your product lines are. Keeping track of price increases will also help you determine if you need to initiate your own price increases during each period, since you need to stay marketable and competitive as often as possible. This type of research is even easier today with inventory access on the internet; just visit your competitor's website for average prices, and make use of search functions for specific products when needed. Signing up for e-mail newsletters and other customer alerts is another way to keep tabs on sales, specials, and other discounts that they may be offering.

2. **Read trade journals, newspapers, and magazines**

   Reading up on industry-related materials is a surefire way to keep track of events, business growth, and even announcement on hirings/firings. Both local and national trade publications can help you tap into a fresh new market, and even find some other companies who you may be able to develop a joint venture with. If you narrow down your competitor research to about 8-10 different companies, glancing through an index or table of contents of each publication for the business is a great way to glean insights on recent activities.

Another to find up-to-date information is in a company blog; blogs are becoming a popular medium with businesses who post recent and upcoming events, and can give you some insights on what's happening 'behind the scenes,' in a timely manner.

3. **Conduct in-depth online research**

   The internet is full of business and company information available to the public domain. Take a look at Hoover's and even Forbes magazine's roundup of company and industry news for accurate data and records of large corporations and companies. From there, you can also determine if the company has a website, traffic and search engine rankings, and how long they've been in business. This is all valuable information on getting some cohesive and comprehensive data on the competition, and can easily be printed and stored for quick reference as you need it. Spending just a few weeks gathering this information can help you assess each company's standing very easily.

   Keeping track of the competition is much easier today with the rich resources of data and public information available on the internet. Creating a tracking system for each of your competitors will help you keep your own records accurate, making it easy to formulate effective goals for growth.

Way to Get Competition Information

Your competition wants to learn about your products, services, customers, trade secrets, and profits. All of these things are relatively easy to uncover, and you should actually be doing the same to them! This is how businesses compete, remain competitive, and improve their product or service, as well as profit margins.

It's a good idea for you to be aware of your competitors' strategies, and how they may find out information about your business. Knowledge is power - and all businesses will use it to their advantage.

The Old Trick - Hire an Ex-Employee

The oldest trick in the book is to hire your former employees. By doing so, they can find out the ins and outs of your business, information about your customers, sales, and new products.

To combat this problem, you should be careful about the kind of information that you disclose to your employees. Divulge information on an as-needed basis, so that they never know more than they need to.

The competition might also ask your customers what they do and don't like about your products and services. When they do this, they are trying to turn your customers against you, which will cause you to lose profits.

Counteract this by assuring your customers that you will always provide good service to them, and that you will reward them for being loyal to you. Then follow up accordingly.

Dirty Tricks in Desperation

Sometimes the competition is afraid of the impact the success of your business has on theirs. Instead of investigating and revising their own plans, they place blame on the competition and never really take control of their own game.

No matter what the situation is, you can learn from their efforts and resolve not to resort to such underhanded tactics. They might try and find out who your vendors are - which is privileged information. When they find out who supplies your products, they might try and persuade those vendors to use their services instead by offering them higher prices or other incentives.

For these reasons, it is important to keep as much information as you can private and out of the wrong hands. You also will need to be as involved as you can in day-to-day operations and business activities. You don't want your business to suffer as a result of their dirty tricks.

Price Wars and More

Advertisements alert your customers that you have a great sale coming up. On the other hand, they also alert the competition to lower their prices as well - which gives customers even more purchasing choices. As you try to expand your business by marketing new and improved products, your competition will also try to do the same thing. These kinds of price and product wars only divide the market.

Spreading negative comments about your product line is another popular tactic aimed at stealing away your customers. To counter this attack, you need to stick to your business plan, make sure your product quality is above reproach and always provide great customer service.

No matter what tricks the competition resorts to, great products and customer service is undeniable - and your customers will see that. Even if your competitors are able to offer lower prices, customers are often willing to pay more for customer service that is second to none.

How to take Advantage of Your Competition?

When people market their business, they pay little attention to their competition. However, they can learn a lot from them. Your competition plays a large role in your business and in your marketing efforts, so don't ignore them.

There is an old saying, "Keep your friends close, keep your enemies closer". In this case, your enemy is your competition. You shouldn't look at your competition as an enemy, but, as a guide or a valuable tool.

Your competition can be an asset to your business. I want you to think about this for a minute, your competition is like having a one stop shopping centre they have it all. Let me give you an example, take a look at your fearsome indirect competition, they have it all. They may have targeted an area of the market that you've missed, on the web that's not hard to do.

1. **Who are their link**

   One day when I was analysing my competition I immediately noticed something about their link partners, a lot of them were different, but some were the same. Let me give you an example, if you were to take three of your competitors, you may only find a few of them with the same link partners, other than that, a large portion of your competition's link partners will be different.

   Once you've found out who your competitor's link partners are, persuade them to link to you. By getting your competition's link partners to link to you, it will take some of your competition's traffic away and give it to you, bringing targeted traffic to your website.

   How do find your competition's link partners? A couple of ways, one is you can use software like Arelis. Arelis will retrieve all the websites that are linked to your competitor in minutes, saving you a boatload of time. Another way to find your competitor's link partners is by using Marketleap's Link Popularity Tool, which is free to use.

2. **Who are their affiliates**

   Another way to take advantage of your competition is to find out who their affiliates are. If you offer an affiliate programme, this may be an ideal strategy for you. Track down your competition's affiliates and persuade them to promote your product or services, instead of your competitor's.

If your competitors offer their affiliates a lower commission percentage than you, then you already have the upper hand. How? Affiliates are always looking for away to make more money and by offering them a higher commission percentage, they'll be able to increase their affiliate profits.

How do you find your competition's affiliates? You can use the same methods to find their affiliates, as you would trying to locate their link partners, by using Arelis and/or Marketleap's Link Popularity Tool.

3. **Spying on your competition**

Thanks to the power of the internet, spying on your competition couldn't be any easier. You can easily find out what their marketing angle is, what they have for products, how much they are charging for their products, and any new products that they may be working on.

If you were to go to your competition offline and evaluate their establishment, while taking notes on their products, you would immediately draw attention to yourself and get thrown out of the store. There is nothing worse than letting your competition know you are keeping tabs on them, but on the internet, it's completely anonymous. Your competition will never know you are there or what you are doing there.

When you pay a visit to your competition's website, the first thing you want to know is, what their weaknesses and their strengths are. That way, you can capitalise on the opportunity of making their weaknesses, strengths.

❑❑❑

9
Techniques To Beat Your Competitors

Understanding your competition is an essential to succeeding. Many times, simply working with the competition can be very profitable for you. Other times, knowing your competition can help you increase your business strategies to keep you in-line, or better than the competition. The old saying, "keep your friends close, but your enemies even closer," also applies in the business world.

Questions to ask yourself when Building your Marketing Plan

Building a proper marketing plan will provide you with the foundation you need to succeed in your business. To build a successful marketing plan, you must ask and answer the right questions.

1. **What is your product or service?**

   This may sound simple, but before you can market your business successfully, you must clearly define what business it is, that you are in. Many an entrepreneur have bit the dust because they simply didn't know what product or service to market. Allow me to ask you this:

   - What product or service are you going to market?
   - Has it previously, or is it currently being marketed successfully?

- What media are your successful competitors using?
- What are their prices?
- In their advertising and marketing, what audience are they targeting?
- Will you be targeting the same audience, meaning how tough will your competition be?

2. **Is there a demand for your product or service?**

Is the projected current demand large enough to justify the costs of research, development, design, packaging, marketing and delivery of your product or service? You must calculate the projected demand against start up, manufacturing, labour and all other costs it will take to get your product or service to your potential customers.

- Is the customer base large enough to support the investment of time and money?
- Is there room to expand?
- Is there a back end sale potential?
- Do you project that your target market will grow, diminish or remain stable?

3. **How can you out do your competitor?**

- Is your product or service of better quality?
- Better price?
- Better service?
- What's your angle?
- If you have competition (which you will 98% of the time), how will your product or service be better?
- How aggressive will your competitors be?

- Will they counter their prices to better their service or product appeal, to beat out yours?
- Can you afford to provide your product or service at a lower rate and still keep a substantial profit margin?

4. **What is your overall strategy?**
    - Will you be targeting one product or service?
    - Will you be targeting a general market or will you require targeting distinct groups of people?
    - Where will you find these people?
    - When considering media, what percentage of the audience fits your target consumer?
5. **How are you employing your tactics?**
    - Have you planned the tactic you will use to accomplish your strategy?
    - What are those special offers that will distinguish you above your competitor?
    - What special services can you provide that they cannot?
    - How will you keep tabs on your competition and their sales rates?
    - How will you collect your fees? Checks or Credit Cards? Online and Offline Solutions?
    - How will you test your product/service against your selected market?
6. **How do you plan to stay on top of things?**
    - How will you track your advertising and promotion?
    - Which promotions and media are drawing the best results?

- Which is the most profitable?
- How can you analyse the demographics to better target your future marketing strategies?
- What networking plans have you made?
- Who do you need to network with and why?
- How will you find and contact them?
- How will you monitor your (broken down) costs versus your profits?
- How will you plan your budget?

7. **What are your future plans?**
   - What is your projected duration for targeted marketing of specific products or services?
   - How will you know when to target new or different products/services?
   - What products and/or services are you planning to add?
   - How can you ensure a safe recovery from failed promotions?
   - How will you know when it's time for your business to grow?
   - How will you delegate authority and who will delegate authority in your absence?
   - What will you do with your success?

Some of these questions may be difficult for you to answer yet, but each should be answered to build that Successful Marketing Plan you need.

Tactics to Overpower Your Competition

To beat your competition, you have to use little techniques that will make you stand out. There are numerous techniques and ideas you can use, but I'm going to show you five important techniques that will help you take your competition by surprise.

1. **To increase** the amount of orders you receive, can be done by changing the price you charge. For example you sell a book for $10. Instead of charging $10 from the customer, charge $9.99 or $9.95. In some cases you can even go up. For example, you could sell a book for $19.95 instead of your original price of $18. Even though this price is higher, you can still receive the same amount of orders or maybe more! The reason why is people will look toward the whole dollar and will not include the cents in their mind. If you are selling something that $10, a $9.95 price tag just sounds better even though it is only five cents cheaper. This is not 'very big change, but it can really help close the sale"

2. **Another technique** is you can use power words. What I'm talking about is words like most powerful, fastest, cheapest, smallest, etc. These types of words usually get more attention, because they are supposedly better than the competition. A good example is motor companies. They can run an ad and say a particular vehicle is the most powerful, roomiest, and fastest car in its class. They are able to say this because of the keyword "in its class". But what people like and want to hear are the power words. The most powerful, roomiest and fastest car. So when the customer searches for a new vehicle, / they will have those ideas in their head, which might be the deciding factor on what vehicle they purchase.

3. **Offering** a time-limited special might decrease your profits or take more time but can give you great success. This extra offer can be savings, free shipping, or an extra-added product or service to the item they

are purchasing. You need to find something that you can offer that is related to your original products or service. I would find something that is as cheap as possible, if not free. Also, put a time limit on this special offer you are giving, because it makes the customer act now, and does not give them time to check out your competition.

4. **Upgrading your service or products** can be very helpful. Try to add new improvements to your products or service and tell your customers what you have done. This will show the customer that your company is determined to keep your service or products up to date with the competition. It will also let them know of all the new features you have added and can be one of the deciding factors they pick in choosing you over your competition.
5. **One idea** very few companies implant is selling a product or service to sell your main products or service. Let's say your main business is the web hosting industry. You can offer a website submission service that will help people promote their website. People will be paying you for this service and you will also have their contact information to offer them your web hosting service. Your website submission service might not bring in a big profit or none at all, but it is targeted to your main business and will give you free leads to new potential customers. You might even want to offer the submission service for free to get more leads.

Highly Effective Marketing Tactics

Here are well known, highly effective marketing tactics many small business owners overlook when developing their marketing programme. How many have you overlooked?

1. **Be unique**

   The best way to beat your competition is to promote a distinct advantage your customers cannot get from a competitor. This is often called your USP (short for Unique Selling Proposition). If you don't already have a distinct advantage, create one. Add something to your business you're not already doing. One network marketer I know doubled her sign up ratio by providing free sales leads to her new distributors for their first four months.

2. **Use testimonials**

   Collect and use testimonials. Testimonials from satisfied customers are similar to referrals. Both provide your prospect with evidence that your product or service produced results for other customers just like them. I've performed many tests using the same messages with and without testimonials. Those with testimonials always increased sales, often by as much as 65% or more.

   Don't wait for satisfied customers to volunteer a testimonial. Instead, follow up with 'some customers soon after completing a transaction. Ask what they liked best about your product, service or business opportunity. You'll get many flattering compliments. Ask for permission to use them in your promotions.

3. **Make An Upselling Offer**

   Upselling is a proven technique you can use to get more money at the point of sale. Customers will never be more receptive to an attractive offer from you than when they're paying you money. Offer your customers or clients the option to upgrade to a better product or service at a special price. Or, offer the option of adding a related item to the sale for a special combination price. Many will accept your offer. An upselling offer can increase your average sale by 30 percent or more without creating any advertising expense.

4. **Trivialise your price**

   Demonstrate a low cost for your product or service by breaking down the price to its lowest time increment. "$325 per year" frightens many customers away. "Enjoy all of this for less than 90 cents a day" attracts them to the low cost.

5. **Stress benefits before features**

   A feature is what something is. A benefit is what it does. For example, my favourite donuts are now delivered in a re-sealable box. That's a feature. The donuts stay fresh for a week after I first open the box. That's the benefit. Promote the benefits of your product or service before you promote the features of it. People never buy something to get a feature. They always buy to get the benefit produced by the feature.

6. **Focus on the headline**

   Always include a headline with your ad, sales letter or webpage. Include your biggest benefit in the headline to grab your prospect's attention. Otherwise, many prospective customers won't read your promotional material. When you develop a new promotion, test different headlines to find the most effective one BEFORE you test anything else. After you find the headline that attracts the most readers you can test to find the most motivating copy for them to read.

7. **Make an offer**

   Never advertise without including an offer. An irresistible offer is the number one reason why people buy something. To substantially increase the response to your advertising, substantially improve your offer. Many small businesses advertise without including an offer. This is a costly mistake because it doesn't provide a reason for prospective customers to respond. The best way to get a big response from your advertising is to make an offer your prospects can't refuse.

Are you using all of these tactics in your promotions? If not, revise your marketing programme to include those you've overlooked. You'll immediately enjoy a big increase in your sales and profits without increasing your expenses.

Beat your Competition without Cutting your Price

One way to beat your competition is to charge less for a similar product or service. But you can also beat your competition when your price is higher. One of the best ways to avoid price competition is to become a specialist in a narrowly defined targeted market.

1. **Relating is more important than pricing**

   I recently spoke with the creator of a marketing programme for new business owners. He could have confronted the established competition and competed with a lower price. Instead he decided to target prospects in 2 types of businesses he had worked with before-insurance sales and MLM marketing (Multi-level Marketing). He knew a lot about the operation of each business and the people who worked in them.

   He created a separate website for each type of business and customised the content to appeal specifically to prospects in that business. The site for insurance sales / people looked the same as the site for MLM marketers. But the content was totally different.

   His plan worked. Sales are running almost 50 percent ahead of projection...even with a price that's 15 percent higher than similar programmes. He built a successful business in a highly competitive market by becoming a specialist.

2. Customers like to buy from a specialist

People like to do business with a specialist who has a unique insight into their situation. They feel confident about getting what they expect from a product or service when it is proposed by somebody who understands them and their unique needs.

Most customers or clients will even pay a little more to buy from somebody who thinks like them. It's worth it to avoid the risk of being disappointed because they bought from somebody who didn't know anything about their special situation.

3. You'll sell more as a specialist

Targeting a niche market enables you to design your sales messages with great precision. You can cater to specifically defined interests of prospects and communicate with them in their own style. More people will buy when they feel you are talking directly to them about their individual needs.

Special Benefit: When you deliver results as a specialist you also establish yourself as an expert in your field. Customers will automatically refer other prospects to you. They value what you did for them. And they're confident you can deliver the same results for others.

4. Three simple steps to becoming a specialist

Becoming a specialist is easier than you may think. You can accomplish it in 3 simple steps:

- Divide your primary market into several narrowly defined markets.

- Take each market, one at a time, and learn everything you can about the prospects in it.
- Revise your marketing approach and selling materials to appeal to the specific needs of prospects in each new market. Use their own unique language and style of communication.

You'll always have competitors. But you don't have to lower your price to compete with them. Instead, become a specialist and cater to prospects in a narrowly defined targeted market. Your understanding and insight into their unique situation will establish you as the expert in your field. They'll want to do business with you even if you don't offer the lowest price.

How to Increase tour Profits with an "Upselling Offer"?

The cost of finding new customers or clients is a big expense for most businesses. "Upselling" those new customers maximises your return on that expense. It's a simple approach any business can implement quickly and get immediate results.

Upselling is a procedure designed to get more money at the point of sale. You implement it by offering your customers or clients an upgraded product or related item at the time they are making their first purchase. Customers will never be more receptive to an attractive offer from you than when they're paying you money. You personally experienced upselling if you ever called to order a product advertised on a TV infomercial. The order taker automatically offered you an additional related product at a special discount only available if you ordered it now.

Many businesses avoid upselling because they're afraid the customer may get irritated and not buy at all.

I've found the opposite is true. Customers appreciate your thoughtfulness in offering them an added benefit they didn't know about. Some business owners have told me they don't upsell because it's not feasible in their business. They really believed that until. I described the upselling offers used successfully by some of their competitors. Every business can implement a successful upselling programme.

Think about your business. What else can you offer customers or clients while they're making their first transaction with you? Can you offer them...

- A discount on a related product or service?
- A volume discount if they buy more now?
- A special priced combination package including the initial product or service?

Your offer should include preferential special pricing. Most customers will accept your upselling offer when it's a good value and the price is no higher than 60% of the cost for the initial product.

How to present an Upselling Offer?

Upselling has none of the characteristics usually associated with selling. It's so easy that I've seen even unskilled order takers achieve high acceptance rates by reading printed scripts. Upselling is simply offering a suggestion to an already receptive buyer to enhance the value of his or her purchase.

Present your upselling offer casually, as almost an afterthought. For example, if you were speaking with your customer in person or by phone you might say: "Your website will be up in 48 hours. If you'd like, we can double your server space, include unlimited autoresponders and a shopping cart for secure credit card orders. The regular price for all of this is an additional $40 per month. But I'll give it to you for just an additional $25 if you order it today." You can make this same offer on paper or post it on website. It doesn't have to be verbal to be effective.

Most businesses I've surveyed report acceptance rates between 40% and 60% for their upselling offers. This is a big increase for so little effort. Plus, the profit from the upselling portion often exceeds the profit on the initial product or service because there are no additional expenses involved.

If you're not making upselling offers to every new customer or client, start doing it now. It's an easy way to boost your profits fast with little effort and no expense.

Magical Words Create Customer Satisfaction and Loyalty

"Man does not live by words alone, despite the fact that sometimes he has to eat them."

How many times have you walked into a store or called a company and received a response that turned up the hair on the nape of your neck? Words are powerful. They can hurt or soothe. Some combination of words creates an immediate negative reaction or image for the receiver of the communication.

"If you can't say something nice, then don't say anything at all." We can hurt our customers and potential customers or have them walk away happy and glad they came into our establishment simply by using words with a positive twist. It is how we combine and state our words and the voice and body inflection we use that can turn a frustrated customer into a happy one.

Let's look at some of the frustrating statements you have heard and discover how through simple rephrasing a negative can be turned into a positive to create satisfied customers.

1. **Hold please!** The phone immediately clicks and the

operator is gone, leaving the client stranded and frustrated. The tone of the operator's voice indicates she is hurried and really does not have time for one more interruption. Customers feel as though they have never had control of the situation and are angered by the receptionist's lack of response to their needs. What if this had been an emergency? A simple "Would you hold please?" would have resolved the situation. Puffing the request in the form of a question allows the customer to feel in control and make a choice to say 'yes' or 'no.'

2. **Well, who is this?** Our gut feeling is to respond by saying "none of your business!" The appropriate question to ask is "Who may I say is calling please?" This places the caller in control of the situation and they can choose whether to disclose their name.

3. **What's this about?** This confrontational question can be restated in a non-threatening manner. "What may I tell him/her this is regarding?" is a much more pleasant question and places the caller at ease. The caller is once more in control of the conversations.

4. **Just a minute and I'll be right back.** The customer is placed in a situation where they have no choice. Whenever possible, give the customer options or ask for permission to take your next action. Try "It might take me a few minutes (or however long it may really take) to find that information. Would you like to hold or can I call you back?"

5. **Well that department is wrong!** This statement places blame on another section or person within the business. It does not represent your company well and is a technique for passing the buck or placing the blame elsewhere. The customer does not care who is wrong, they just want the situation corrected regardless

of where the mistake was made. "Let me see how I can fix this for you," shows a willingness to rectify the situation and places the customer at ease. It is an immediate tension reliever and begins to dissipate a customer's angry feelings.

6. **It's back there someplace** is not the response a customer wants when they ask where they can find an item. Maybe the customer has just walked the aisle five times and still cannot find the product they want. Or maybe this is the first...and quite possibly the last.. time they have been in your store and they have no idea where the different departments are located. You have three choices when asked the location of a product. The first and best response is "let me show you." TI, however, you are unable to take the customer to the item, then give them a complete description of where the item can be found: "It's on aisle 5, about halfway back, right side, lower shelf." If you do not know the location then be honest and find out. "Good question. Let me get someone who can show/tell you."

7. **We can't do that** will put a wall of defensiveness up as fast as any statement. Remember to tell the customer what you can do, not what you can't. "That's a great question. We can..." is more pleasant to hear and gives the customer alternatives to select from.

8. **It's the company policy.** Customers do not care what the organisational policies or rules are. Remember, 95% of the policies are made for 5% of the customers that will always ask for the exception. "Normally we don't do that. In your case, I'll gladly make an exception." This really makes the client feel special. It lets them know it is not the normal company policy and yet there are always exceptions to the rules and a willingness to satisfy the customer's needs.

9. **It's not my job**. The customer really doesn't care whose job it is. They just want a situation rectified. "I'll be glad to help you," or "let me get someone from that department to help you" indicates willingness on your part to either help or get assistance for the individual.
10. **That can't happen,** is like telling the customer they are lying. Even though you believe the situation did not occur, you will never have exactly the same experience as the customer. We all experience a given situation differently because of our past and our perceptions of a given situation. To place the customer at ease, try "I apologize (or I'm sorry) you had that experience. Let me see how I can fix it."
11. **You have to have..,** is a demand, not a request. Our schedules limited my soon to be husband and I to one specific day to apply for our marriage license within the allotted time period. After driving an hour to the county seat and standing in line for 45 minutes, we were told we did not have all the correct documents. We were frustrated. The staff member had not provided that information when we called about the process. There were no exceptions! We returned home, drove back again and got our license 30 minutes before closing. A better way to approach a request is, "We want to help you. Can you provide us with – ?" If the customer's response is no, then begin to explore alternatives or other avenues for obtaining the information.
12. **It's the computer's fault.** The individual who does the data entry is not a computer. So who really made the mistake, the computer or the person?

    When blame is placed on an object, it is just as bad as blaming another person or department. The customer wants resolution to the problem. Apologize and move on. "I'm sorry you had this experience. Let me see how I can correct it for you."

Words can send an upset customer into orbit. When sincerely stated, words can also soothe and express that you are ready to help and serve. Review some of the phrases you use when speaking with customers. Are your words magic to their ears or do they come crashing down leaving the customer frustrated, defensive and angry? Select your words and phrases wisely and you too will calm the raging client and win loyal customers, and customers who refer you business.

Easy Ways to Increase Sales — Fast

What am I doing wrong?" That's a question business owners often ask themselves when business is slow. Often, the answer is... "You're not doing anything wrong. You just need to do some things better -- and you need to start doing a few things you've been neglecting." Here's a list you can use to evaluate your own marketing efforts. It includes most important marketing principles contributing to the success of any business.

1. **Target specific niche markets**

   Everyone may be a prospect for your product or service. But your marketing efforts will produce the best results for the lowest cost when you target prospects with the greatest need for what you offer. Identify a niche market. Customise your promotional material to appeal to their greatest need. Then multiply your results by defining several other niche markets and slanting your promotional materials to appeal to the biggest need of prospects in each market.

2. **Promote your own USP**

   USP is short for "Unique Selling Proposition". It's the compelling reason why a prospect will do business with you instead of with your competition. You'll attract the maximum number of customers when you offer a benefit they cannot get from your competitors. If you don't already have a USP, create one by adding something to your business you're not already offering. Convert it into a benefit statement and include that statement in all your advertising.

3. **Never advertise without an offer**

   Always include a powerful offer in your advertising. Offer free information related to your product or service to generate inquiries or website traffic. Then make the most compelling discount or bonus offer you can afford--to convert these inquiring prospects into paying customers. This automatically leads to the next marketing principle...

4. **Collect contact information and use it to follow up**

   Most prospects won't buy the first time they hear or see your sales message. You need a system to collect contact information enabling you to reach them again with periodic reminders and offers. Many businesses develop over 50 percent of their sales by following up with prospects who previously requested information but didn't buy--yet. Advertising is expensive. Maximise your return on it by following up periodically with the prospects it produced to convert more of them into customers.

5. **Remove the obstacle of risk**

   Do you know the major reason why people don't buy something they want or need? They don't want to take the chance of getting something different than they expect and maybe even losing money. You can eliminate this risk by guaranteeing satisfaction. If you sell products, offer a liberal money back guarantee. If you provide a service, offer to continue working without additional charge until the promised result is achieved.

6. **Diversify**

   It's easier and less expensive to get more business from satisfied customers than to find new customers. Continually find or develop new products and services related to what you sell -- and offer them to your customers. Affiliate programmes offer a quick and low-cost way for Internet based businesses to add new products and services to their inventory.

7. **Never stop testing**

   Continually test and evaluate the effectiveness of everything you use or do to promote business. Here's a highly effective 80/20 guideline you can use. Invest 80 percent of your advertising budget and effort in proven promotions and 20 percent in testing new variations. Most businesses using this system continue growing--even in a highly competitive market.

Take a few minutes to evaluate how well you're implementing each of these seven marketing principles in your business. A small improvement in just one of them will boost your sales immediately. An improvement in several will generate a big increase in your total sales volume.

Increase your Sales by Reversing the Risk

You may be losing a lot of business without knowing it. It happens every time a potential customer decides not to buy from you because they may not get all they expect from your product or service. You can save much of this lost business by reversing that risk. One way to reverse the risk is to guarantee every claim you make. For example, tell your prospects:

"If for any reason (product or service) doesn't deliver every claim or promise we made, we'll refund 100% of what you paid."

You'll be amazed at how much more business you'll get with this simple guarantee. Reversing the risk breaks down your customer's resistance and instills confidence that your claims must be true. It enhances your credibility because you certainly wouldn't guarantee a full refund if your product or service didn't deliver as promised.

Maybe you're reluctant to provide a money back guarantee because you're afraid some people may take unfair advantage of it. I've learned by experience that you don't have to worry about refunds if you offer a quality product or service at a fair price. The buyers who take advantage of a money back guarantee represent only a tiny percentage of the total increased business generated by the guarantee.

1. **Make your offer better than risk free**

   Did you ever decide to buy something then change your mind at the last minute? Maybe you even had your cheque book or credit card out but stopped at the very last second. Some of your potential customers do this. You can convert many of these "almost sales" into customers by offering a guarantee enhanced with a bonus. TV infomercials use this technique all the time. You can copy it to increase sales in your business.

   To use this technique, add something extra to your offer as a bonus and tie it into your guarantee. If your customer is dissatisfied and uses your guarantee, he or she can return the product or cancel the service and get a full refund. But, they don't have to return the bonus item. Now your offer is better than risk free. This "free bonus you can keep" motivates many "almost buyers" to take action and become customers.

   Sometimes you can offer a guarantee your customer automatically gets from somebody else. It may be a guarantee from the manufacturer or even a legally required guarantee. For example, most states require life insurance companies to refund 100% of the premiums paid when a policy is returned within 10 days after delivery. Many insurance agents persuade prospective buyers to submit an application with the premium payment based on this guarantee. This is a good example of a guarantee provided by somebody else (government regulators). It's also an excellent example of reversing the risk from the buyer to the seller.

2. **Reversing the risk for a service business**

   Removing the risk by providing a money back guarantee works well when a product is involved. But, how do you provide a guarantee when the transaction involves a service? Your customer can't return yesterday's plumbing job. The work was already performed.

   Instead of offering a money back guarantee, a service business can provide a guarantee to solve the customer's problem. For example, our plumber in the example above can guarantee to come back without charge as often as necessary to stop the leak. A landscaper can replace without charge any plants that don't survive for at least 6 months. A sales consultant can continue working without charge until the promised sales results are achieved.

3. **Reversing the risk for a business opportunity**

   Nobody can guarantee someone-else's success in operating a business. But, there are some things you can do to lower the buyer's risk.

   If you offer a MLM (Multi-level Marketing)/Network Marketing business opportunity, your company is responsible for any guarantees involving their products or services. However, you can lower the business risk for your new distributors by offering support in sales and recruiting. For example, you can:

- Provide free prospect leads.
- Recruit their first few distributors.
- Conduct 3-way conference calls to help persuade their prospects to sign up.
- Provide free recruiting postcards.

Any sales or recruiting support you offer reduces the business risk and convinces more people to sign up under you.

Start thinking about some of the things you can do in your business to reverse the risk for your potential customers and clients. Then implement them and watch how fast your sales and profits increase

Creating Customers for Life

In growing gardens we often think about the process of planting seed and fertilizing and cultivating the soil. The same is true of your prospects and clients. In a society where people are pressed for time and pulled in many different directions, it's vitally important that you keep your name in front of them.

By cultivating your prospects and clients, you build longterm, mutually profitable relationships that are so critical in order for them to see you as a resource. Cultivation of your prospects and clients accomplishes three things:

- It conditions people to buy. By staying in touch with them, you are able to identify their needs so that they want to do business with you.
- It establishes who you are in the mind of the prospect. With all the messages they are receiving and the number of financial advisors that are trying to approach them,

cultivation will differentiate you and help you stand out.

- It lowers resistance to your ideas, products, and services. By becoming aware of who you are over a period of time, prospects will begin to see the value of what you do and clients will be more likely to purchase additional products and services from you.

There are many ways to inform and inspire your clients and prospects, however, in order to reach them on a regular basis you should maintain an accurate list of information about them. Today's computer technology makes it easy to load all your targeted prospects and clients into a database. Enter each person's name with a market code, record the date entered along with any special dates such as birthdays, purchase dates, or business anniversaries. You could also include the mail you've sent or telephone calls you've made in their record. Having this information in a database makes it easy- for you to stay close to your niche market prospects and customers. You can communicate with them through the ways they associate and communicate with one another. You can gain access faster by timing and tailoring your information message to match your market segments. To move forward, ask yourself how you can inform and inspire and cultivate the prospects and clients in your targeted niche markets. The following tactics are designed to help you answer that question.

1. **Send articles of interest to your prospects and customers**

Look for articles of interest in various magazines, newspapers, and general-interest periodicals. Obtain permission to reproduce them, and send them to your target market prospects and clients. There are really two criteria for success with this tactic:

- The article should inform your readers about their industry, interests, or recreational activities.
- It should be accompanied by a simple note card that says, "I thought this would be of interest to you." You could also use a Post-it note to make it appear even more personalized.

Sending articles not only informs, it shows your interest in prospects and customers. In turn, this stimulates their interest in you.

2. **Create a list of 20 ways to make your prospect's life or business better**

   Send this list to the prospects and customers in your niche. A marketing, sales, or other business idea that furthers their sales or profits is always welcome. In recreational market segments, golf tips or tennis tips would be helpful, as would school safety ideas, or fundraising or meeting ideas for special-interest segments.

3. **Inspire prospects and send them a thank-you note for saying no**

   When individuals don't buy from you now, that doesn't necessarily mean they won't buy sometime in the future. Let them know that you're always open to work with them, irrespective of present circumstances. A thank-you note for saying no could be something as simple as, "Disappointed we're unable to do business now. Look forward to working with you in the future. Always feel welcome to call." A thank you for saying no helps open closed doors in the future. After sending the note, call back in 30 days and ask how things are proceeding. You'll often find that prospects are still uncommitted. As a result, the door of opportunity will reopen.

4. **Send a thank-you note after the sale to inspire future business**

   Frequently after a sale, agents simply say "thank you," shake hands, walk out the door, and move on to the next sale. Remember, a thank-you note sent to the decision maker helps continue your relationship and ensures future access and sales.

5. **Send a personal note to inspire**

   A lesson learned from former President George Bush. Each day, send a warm and friendly note to 50 to 100 of your prospects and clients. Omit any sales literature; just send a personal tone that cultivates, informs, and inspires. It should be no longer than three sentences or it becomes a letter that requires an opening, middle, and a close. Mention something interesting, or simply give them a word of encouragement. It will demonstrate that you value their business in a personal way. These notes, over a lifetime, enabled George Bush to create support for his nomination as Ronald Reagan's Vice President.

6. **Be sure your voice mail message informs and inspires**

   Be sure that your greeting is not just a dry, cumbersome "leave a message at the sound of the tone." Instead, use your greeting as an informative message about your practice that, at the same time, encourages the individual that has called you. For example, "I'm so glad you called. I look forward to making a difference in your financial picture. Please leave your name and number at the sound of the tone, and I will return your call either later today or first thing in the morning."

Finally, pay attention to little things. Because value today is determined by the buyer and not the seller, it's the little things that make a difference, particularly in relation to how you build a mutually rewarding, long-term relationship with them. It's not just how well a brochure or mailer is designed or how professional it looks. Sometimes it's just the fact that you've taken the minute to write someone that counts. It's the cup of coffee that you buy, it's the chocolate or cashews that you bring to the secretary, it's the thank-you notes you send, it's asking about the children, it's finding out about how wife or husband is doing, it's telling someone you're going to pray for them and then letting them know you have; it's all these little things that make a difference. All these things help people in your niche markets know you in a special way. We know that people are less brand-loyal that we must concentrate on it we want to cultivate and grow our business and theirs.

Keys to Attracting more Clients

It's always easier to attract the things we want in life than to chase them down and catch them. The old saying, "You catch more flies with honey than with vinegar."

One of the things many professionals and small business owners want is "more clients". While there are lots of strategies for getting clients, from advertising to workshops, one of the best (and fastest) is to be the type of person and provide the quality service that draws clients to you like flies to honey! The following Principles for Attracting Great Clients are:

- Become incredibly selfish: Yes, it's ironic, but as you take care of yourself, manage your time, your space and your life well, you have more to give and more to share. If you want more clients, take extremely good care of Clients.
- Over-respond to every event: This is the opposite

of over-reacting. Respond immediately to phone calls, answer questions in full, take your time and thoughtfully and creatively go the extra mile.

- Add value just for the joy of it: Do more, provide more, go further than you are paid for. Caution: Don't just give more stuff, give more stuff that people really want and appreciate.
- Market your talents shamelessly: Have fun with your marketing, be proud of what you do. Laugh and joke and yell and whisper, but tell everybody! If you aren't excited, proud and energised by what you do, find another job!
- Affect others profoundly: Abandon the roles and job descriptions we all have. Connect with people, question, respond, be silly, get "outside the box." Whatever it takes, make an impact on your world.
- Eliminate delay: Time is expensive, and wasting it is unattractive and irritating. Think and plan carefully, but in the end, only action counts.
- Thrive on the details: Pay attention to the subtleties, the small things. It's the little extras that build you up, and little slips that bring you down.
- Tolerate nothing: Clean up all the irritations, the daily frustrations and predictable annoyances of your life once and for all! Don't just fix the problem, re-design your routine so those predictable irritations never bother you again.
- Orient life around your values: When you spend your days living in harmony with your values, you become incredibly energised, peaceful, focused and attractive.
- Develop more character than you need: Beyond being good at your job, and living with integrity, become

very good at being YOU! Be a "real character", the unique, gifted, complex and unforgettable individual that you were born to be.

Think about the idea that your professional relationship with a client must begin with a good personal relationship. When your clients experience you as a balanced, open, excited person who they enjoy being with. ..they'll tell their friends.

Difference between: What the customers need and what they want?

A widely held belief is that people buy products or services. There is also an even more widely held misconception that people buy what they need. The real truth is that people buy the end result that they want rather than the product or service they may need. There is also a big difference between a salesperson being Needs based and Needs obsessed!

To put it differently, people will eagerly buy what they need from the salesperson or organisation who understands what they really want. As the old adage puts it, a lot more beer is sold than Bibles! There are also a lot more sugar-coated cookies consumed than bran muffins. A lot of 4-wheel drive vehicles are sold in West Texas. A place where people certainly don't "Need" 4-wheel drives.., they just want them.

Let me ask you a perplexing question. One that lots of people have difficulty answering. And here it is: What is the real difference between what a prospect Needs and what that person Wants?

In observing over 7,000 sales interactions, we discovered that prospects actually verbalised what they wanted less than .01% of the time. The reason for it is simple. Most people don't know what they Want.

Here's why. Wants are below the surface while Needs are above the surface. I know I Need a new car. However, I will ultimately buy the one I Want! The feeling or emotion behind owning it is what I Want. Needs are totally rational while Wants are purely emotional. Needs are based on fact while Wants are grounded on perception. Needs are product or service specific while Wants have very little, if anything, to do with the product or service being offered.

A few good questions about what customers really Want...

- Do prospects like small talk?

  Fact: Over 74% of customers dislike unsolicited small talk by salespeople.

  Prospect Want: "We'll talk if I want to."

- Will prospects tell you they don't want to engage in small talk?

  Fact: Less than 0.8% will tell you that it bothers them.

  Prospect Want: "I won't tell you I don't like you. I just won't buy."

- Do customers trust salespeople?

  Fact: 64% of all buyers say they don't trust any of the salespeople they've bought something from in the previous 24 month period.

  Prospect Want: "Salespeople I can trust."

- Should salespeople change their title to "consultant" or "advisor?"

  Fact: 72% of prospects perceive words like "consultant" or "advisor" to be slick or manipulative.

  Prospect Want: "Straightforward, professional salespeople."

- What do prospects remember?

Fact: When the average decision-maker doesn't buy, he or she remembers fewer than 10 words (verbatim) spoken by a salesperson doing a presentation.

Prospect Want: "Give me a presentation I can understand."

- How persistent should you be?

  Fact: 74% of decision-makers feel that persistence is not an admirable trait for salespeople.

  Prospect Want: "Leave me alone. I'll buy from you when and if I want to."

- How "data dense" are most sales presentations?

  Fact: The average salesperson presents 6-8 features or benefits in a sales presentation. Twenty-four hours later the average prospect remembers one. In 39% of the cases they remember it incorrectly. In 49% of the cases they remember something that wasn't mentioned at all!

  Prospect Want "A product that does what I want it to do, explain in my terms."

What does all this mean? Quite simply this: prospects and customers are far different from the way that most salespeople traditionally perceive them as being. The secret is to intake prospects feel good and then to be there when they feel so good that they'll buy! When they feel like that they'll buy again and again.

What kind of person talks too much?

Our survey of 1,311 decision-makers revealed one, singular answer. It was simple and straightforward: salespeople! The solution to this is simple. Talk less, ask more questions. Sell people what they Want.. . offer them what they Need.

Super-Practical Steps to Build Your Business

For the past several weeks, we have focused on some wonderful but rather fancy ideas about life. Its include tips for help in actually running your office from day to day. So, let's talk about some practical steps that clients have used to build their referral business quickly and systematically. Let's walk through it.

- **Step: 1**

  Take care of, cleanup, and get rid of 5 tolerations in your office or work. Make a list! Look around your space, your car, your desk or office, and commit to spending an hour taking care of at least 5 small, daily annoyances that have been bugging you, robbing your energy, or making life difficult. Do that filing! Repair that broken light, or throw out those old magazines. Buy a new desk chair, or a whole new desk! You can't afford to be distracted by these things. Fix them.

- **Step: 2**

  Contact 5 former clients or customers. Send them a letter, call them, and even send those flowers or a small gift in cases where that might be appropriate. Invite them back, offer them a free follow-up or consultation. Ask them to help you evaluate your service by completing a questionnaire or ask them to come in for an interview. Tell them you value them as customers and want them to come back - and refer their friends!

- **Step: 3**

  Contact 5 current clients. Follow a similar routine from Step: 2. Call them up, or send a card or letter telling them they are valued customers. Invite their comments on how you can improve your service or expand your business. Let them know you appreciate their trust and value their ideas. Do it nicely, with tact and sincerity, but ask them to help you build your business.

- **Step: 4**

  Contact 5 potential customers or clients who have never used your services, and make them an offer they have to respect. Go through your rolodex, your list of friends, colleagues, associates and members of organisations you belong to - use the Yellow Pages if you have to-but pick up that phone and invite 5 people to check you out! If it's appropriate, tell them you want to grow your business and offer them a free sample (who could turn down a free massage or a free oil change, or....?) If that's not appropriate, tell them you want to grow your business and you'd love to meet with them, buy them lunch, whatever it takes. You've been practicing for two days, so you know you can do this.

- **Step: 5**

  This is the hardest one of all: Do 5 wonderful things for yourself! You've worked hard all week, taken risks, put the word out that you are ready and eager to handle more business. That means you need to be healthy, energised, relaxed and ready. So, go for a walk, take a long lunch and visit a friend. Read a great novel - or a trashy one, your choice! Enjoy the sunshine, or relax and listen to the rain. Spoil a neighbour kids, and then give them back!

This week, take some specific, measured steps to create more room and build your business. If you wanted practical, this is it. Now, it's your choice.

Using Advertising for a Competitive Advantage in Business

One method to gain an advantage in a business competition is through strategic use of advertising. Good marketing and advertising makes people aware of what products or services a business has to offer. It is used to bring in potential customers. Special advertising strategies can be used to gain the upper hand. You can win sales by doing a better job at advertising than your opponents, by attacking them in your ads, or even preventing them from advertising. But also, the competition may be doing the same thing, so a defensive plan must also be in place.

Questions you may have include:

1. How do you do better in advertising than competition?
2. How effective are advertising attacks?
3. How can a business prevent others from advertising?

Having Better Ads

The most common way for a company to beat the competition in reaching the public and gaining their attention is through doing a better job in advertising. This includes using clever ads, focusing on specific markets, and purchasing more advertising space than the opponents.

Your performance in advertising is what gives you the advantage. Although clever advertising can catch the eye of the public, the product still must be good in order to keep the customers.

Attacking Opponent in Ads

Some companies have used comparison ads to show their product is superior as compared to the competition. They will show comparisons and state statistics. This is using advertising for an advantage in a head-to-head competition.

The problem with this strategy to beat the opponent in advertising is that it gives the opponent free exposure and name recognition. But it can still create a negative perception of the product among the public.

Preventing Opponent from Advertising

In most situations, it is difficult to prevent competitors from advertising effectively. But there are examples of such a strategy being used effectively:

1. Large companies have been known to pressure the media into not displaying ads of smaller competitors.
2. In political campaigns, there have been many cases where a candidate for office removed opponent's signs and replaced them with his.
3. Some companies have had people illegally deface the ads of the competition.

Companies can use advertising strategies to gain a competitive advantage. The company can win by doing a better job at advertising than opponents, attacking them in the ads, or even preventing them from advertising.

How to use Outsourcing to Beat Your Competition?

Outsourcing is when you hire outside professionals or services to take on part of your business workload. You may want to outsource part of your work because you don't have the room, you need an expert, you have periodic busy periods, or you need more production to get orders out on time etc. You could outsource accounting, secretarial tasks, factory help, computer training, web design etc. Below are ways to use outsourcing to beat your competition.

By outsourcing part of your workload you can save time and spend more time concentrating on beating your competition.

- you won't have to take time training new employees
- you won't have to do time consuming tasks like adding on new equipment
- you won't have to learn a new software program or other equipment
- you won't have to interview employee candidates
- you won't have to fill out all the complicated employee paper work like tax forms, scheduling, retirement plans etc.

By outsourcing part of your workload you can save money and spend more money on marketing or advertising to beat your competition.

- you won't have to buy extra office and other equipment
- you won't have to buy extra office or work space
- you won't have spend money on employee costs like; taxes, medical, vacation time, holidays, workers comp., unemployment costs etc. (these may vary by which country you do business)

There are many other ways outsourcing can help you beat your competition. Here are a few more:

- the extra help can help you complete and deliver orders faster
- you could expand your market share by becoming the middleman and offering your subcontractors services or products
- you could end up getting orders from your subcontractors
- it will allow your business to take on extra or large orders

Winning the Business Competition: Mapping Your Company's Competitive Awareness

Commerce is a competition, and each business is a competitor. In all the theories and tools around business management and strategic planning, not nearly enough emphasis is put on the competitive element of business. A tool is attached which owner, managers can use, together with their key employees and advisors, to ensure that their business plans contain strong dose of competitive thinking. Some background notes on the tool are set out below.

Business is a Competition

- The goal of this competition is to impose your vision of products and services onto a marketplace which includes competitors, suppliers and customers, thereby tapping into the purchasing power of targeted consumers in that marketplace for personal profit.
- The competition is characterized by the pursuit of personal profit using limited economic resources.
- The attributes of the competition include hostility, chaos, friction, uncertainty, continuous change and disorder.

The attached mapping tool will help you think about your business and your business plan as a competitor in a business competition, and will help you move from a strategic/visionary view of your business to a list of specific and measurable deliverables.

- **Step 1**
  Competitive Positioning – Visionary Thinking

  Our market, our place in the market, and how we must be perceived by ourselves, our customers, our suppliers and our competitors to be competitive in the long run.

Every plan must begin with a vision, a sense of final result, a statement of what you are trying to be and why, and how you are going to do it. There must be a winning vision. It must recognise that there is a competition going on, and that the goal of the competition is to "win" at some level. The vision must encompass the whole marketplace - customers, suppliers, competitors - and sustain success for you and your business in the long run.

- **Step 2**
  Competitive Focus — Vision Meets Strategy

  What we will focus on in the near future to secure our place in the market as against our competitors. In developing competitive focus and strategic objectives, the attributes of business competition must be kept clearly in mind, including the need for personal profit and the lack of unlimited financial resources to pursue that need.

  All strategies must recognise the competition itself by imposing your vision onto the marketplace. Seizing initiative and forcing others to react to your lead will greatly improve your chances of succeeding in the competition.

  In setting strategic objectives, a key understanding of weaknesses is necessary, both yours and your competitors'. Attacking their weaknesses through your strengths, while being mindful of defending your own weaknesses, tells you what to do, how to do it, and what resources you need to get the job done. That requires a frank and honest assessment of your own abilities and position in the competition.

- **Step 3**
  Competitive Success Factors — Strategy Meets Management

What we must accomplish in the short run to maintain our focus and fulfil our competitive vision in our market.

With competitive positioning and focus in mind, short term accomplishment must be clearly and specifically defined, and resources found and allocated to fulfil those accomplishments.

"Control" is managed by setting a clear list of accomplishments and objectives in a way that fosters knowledge of what needs to be done in a broad sense as well as a winning attitude. People need know what they have to do and why, and what resources they have to get their part done, without a lot of interference in how they do it. In return for a certain degree of freedom to operate, team members must accept responsibility for their decisions and be accountable. Initiative is balanced with responsibility.

Subordinates must also become responsible for "lateral coordination". They must integrate their actions and objectives with others who are in the same chain of command. Each has knowledge of the company's overall competitive position and focus, as well as their own competitive success factors. Rather than going up the line to get direction on how to get things done, they are expected to work together, and only go up the line if there is disagreement or misunderstanding as to focus or vision.

By hiring, developing and empowering similar types of people throughout the organisation, people of initiative and imagination who accept responsibility and accountability, and who are required and capable of working together, and by delegating vision objectives and not methods, owner managers can ease their own burdens, concentrate on the areas where they should be spending their energies, and can benefit from a stronger, more vibrant and more proactive organisation.

- **Step 4**
  Measuring Deliverables – Management Meets Strategy

  How we are going to know that we are achieving our objectives, maintaining our focus and fulfilling our vision.

  Success must be measured. Without measurement there is insufficient accountability. Without measurement, decisions to stay the course or take corrective action may be made too late in the competition. Without measurement, jumping in at the right time with the right help can not be done. Defining what to measure, when to measure, and what to do with those results, and tying it all in back in through competitive success factors, completive focus and competitive positioning- from management through strategy to vision - is essential to being and staying competitive.

Top 3 Ways to Beat the Competition

It's inevitable that your retail business will have some form of competition. And while you can't control what your competitors do, you can minimise their impact on your business. Here are three ways to rise above the competition.

Reduce Expenses, not Advertising

Take a look at your Profit and Loss statement, or itemize all of your expenses, and ask yourself how each line can be eliminated or reduced. Find out where you can cut back. A little here and a little there will soon add up. However, the one expense you do NOT want to reduce is advertising. In fact, many retailers will increase their marketing efforts during slower sales periods because there is more competition and fewer consumer dollars.

Reducing Retail Business Expense

There may come a time when a retailer is faced with the need to cut expenses. It could be a slump in the economy or the threat of a new competitor. Or it may simply be the desire to control those ever-expanding monthly operating expenditures.

Whatever the reason, there are areas in spending in which retailers can reduce without compromising customer service or quality. If your store is experiencing a cash crunch, consider the following ways to cut retail business expenses.

Begin looking at the store's budget to find areas that can be cut out completely or considerably trimmed back. List every expense the business incurs, all the way down to cash register paper, and then determine where the shop can save money.

Buying in bulk, buying used and comparison shopping are all options for saving money. Every bit adds up. Keep in mind that many business expenses can be negotiated for better rates or terms. With a little planning and some research, retailers may find better services for less.

Areas to Reduce Expenses

- Credit card processing fees
- Telephone and utility bills
- Internet and web hosting
- Professional fees
- Banking Services
- Postage and shipping fees
- Office supplies and equipment

- Overtime pay
- Health Plans
- Business insurance

Instead of trimming costs here and there, what if your retail business really needs to slash expenses? Before you go hacking necessary sales tools, like advertising and staffing, consider cutting completely any item that is not required to stay in business. Be careful, the idea is to cut any unnecessary expenses, not sacrifice efficiency or professionalism.

Items your Business may Survive without

- Cell phones
- Donations
- Magazine subscriptions
- Trade organisations
- Professional dues
- Landscaping
- Sanitorial service

Plan ahead, create a realistic budget and get the entire staff involved. Employees are more willing to help store owners control expenses when they understand the next cut could be their own job.

Get Creative

Retailers in the same industry generally use similar marketing methods to reach customers. Now is the time to get creative and use unconventional marketing methods to distinguish your business from the competition. A unique marketing campaign attracts more attention and lands more sales. Also, look for some new untapped market you and your competitors overlooked. You may uncover a niche market you can dominate with lithe or no competition.

Some Marketing Ideas for Retailers

Small business owners can easily get too involved in the day-to-day operations of their retail stores to spend any time brainstorming marketing ideas or promotional events. Some retailers worry that marketing is too expensive, others may find it too time consuming. Without announcing who you are and what you sell, how will anyone know? Here are some marketing ideas for retailers.

- Create a calendar for customers with your shop's name and address on it.
- Print the products you sell or services offered on the back of your business cards.
- Always carry business cards with you. Give them freely and ask permission to leave them in places your target market may visit.
- Join a trade association or organisation related to your industry.
- Have a drawing for a product or a gift certificate. Use the entry forms to collect customers' mailing addresses.
- Develop a brochure of services your shop offers.
- Conduct monthly clinics about a product or service you offer or schedule semi-annual seminars on related "how-to" information for your industry.
- Print a tagline for your business on letterhead, fax cover sheets, e-mails and invoices.
- Develop a website to showcase your products, services and location. Use a memorable URL and include it on all marketing materials.
- Include customer testimonials in your printed literature.

- Promote yourself as an expert by writing articles or tips on topics related to your industry.
- Submit to the local newspaper, trade journal or other publications.
- Host an after-hours gathering for your employees and their friends/ relatives.
- Provide free t-shirts with your logo to your staff to wear.
- Send newsworthy press releases as often as needed.
- Create an annual award and publicise it.
- Develop your own TV show on your specialty and present it to your local cable station or public broadcasting station.
- Create a press kit and keep its contents current.
- Use an answering machine or voice mail system to catch after-hours phone calls. Include basic information in your outgoing messages such as business hours, location, website, etc.
- Join a Chamber of Commerce where you can network with area business owners.
- Hold an open house. Invite prominent city officials and the press.
- Get a memorable local or toll-free phone number.
- Place ads in publications your market reads. Be sure to reach the non-English speaking market as well.
- Distribute specialty products such as pens, mouse pads, or mugs with your store's logo.
- Advertise in creative locations such as park benches, buses, and popular Websites.
- Improve your building signage.

- Get a booth at a trade show or expo attended by your target market.
- Give a speech or volunteer for a career day at a high school.
- Sponsor and Adopt-a-Highway area in your community to keep roads litter-free.
- Donate your product or service to a charity event or auction.
- Have a Yellow Pages ad listed under your main industry and in related categories.
- Volunteer your time to a charity or non-profit organisation.
- Create a loyalty programme to reward existing customers.
- Create an opt-in e-mail or print newsletter for your customers. Fill each edition with specials, tips and other timely information.
- Send hand-written thank you notes to important customers every chance you get.
- Use brightly coloured envelopes and unique stationary when sending direct mail pieces.
- Show product demos or related videos on a television on the sales floors during store hours.
- Book a celebrity guest for an event at your store. Use people in your industry or television news anchors or local authors.
- Create window displays in locations away from your shop. Airports, hospitals, and large office buildings occasionally have display areas they rent to local businesses.

- Team up with a non-competing business in your area to offer a package promotion.
- Pick the slowest day of the week to hold a one-day sale.
- Create a warm, welcoming waiting area for your customers.
- Provide extra customer service training for your staff.
- Sign up for a newsletter or join online discussion groups in your industry.
- If possible, loan your facilities to other groups for a meeting place.
- Create a unique lapel pin based on the products you sell to wear at meetings.
- Choose a regular customer to spotlight as a Customer of the Month. Create a brief write up to submit to the local newspaper about the customer and be sure to give he or she a copy of the article as well as have one framed to hang in the store.
- Pair up slow moving items with related products and repackage as a special buy.
- Start a blog. Write about your industry or detail in-store happenings.
- Offer your customers discounts for each referral they provide.

Marketing is most effective if done in coordination with other exposure. Enhance the above efforts with additional signage, newspaper ads, displays and radio ads. Remember to tailor each event for your target audience. If your message isn't being delivered to the right person, it may be a wasted effort.

Providing Outstanding Customer Service

By going the extra mile to provide good service, retailers can outlast the competition. Make shopping in your store such a memorable experience that customers can't wait to come back or to tell their friends. People like to shop where they feel comfortable and where they feel the owner truly cares about their wants and needs.

As individuals, we all have our own little pet peeves. What may turn off one customer may not bother another. As retailers, we can't afford to turn off a single customer and image is everything. Keeping our stores neat and clean is not only easy to do; it is generally an inexpensive way to attract customers and create a pleasant store atmosphere.

Take a look around your retail store. Do any of the following situations exist? Here are ten ways your store may be turning off customers:

1. **Dirty bathrooms**

   This customer pet peeve clearly deserves the number one spot on this list. Retail store restrooms should always be sparkling clean, whether they are open for public use or not. Make sure to stock the bathrooms with plenty of paper products, soap, trash receptacles and clean it daily.

2. **Messy dressing rooms**

   Keeping the dressing room area free of discarded hangers, tags and empty packaging goes beyond creating a neat store appearance, it is also a good step towards loss prevention. Take a quick look for out of place items after each customer uses the dressing room.

3. **Loud music**

   Playing music in a retail store can help create a certain atmosphere for our shoppers. Music that is too loud, inappropriate or of poor quality can run a positive shopping experience.

4. **Handwritten signs**

In this era of technology, there is no excuse for displaying handwritten signage. It is too simple to print a sign from our computers or use pre-printed signs. Printed signs simply look more professional and signs with hard-to- read handwriting can be a customer turn-offers.

5. **Stained floor or ceiling tiles**

It is true, accidents happen. However, our customers don't have to see them. Dirty carpet, stained flooring and ugly ceiling tiles can turn off many shoppers. Sweeping, vacuuming and mopping should be done on a regular basis. Consider hiring a professional cleaning crew to polish tile floors. Replace stained portions of carpet and ceiling tiles where possible.

6. **Burned-out or poor lighting**

Replace any burned out light bulbs as soon as possible. Make sure all customer areas of the store have ample lighting and take into consideration shoppers with aging or less than perfect eyesight. Your store should be well illuminated for all customers.

7. **Offensive odours**

Customers understand if they visit a lawn and garden centre will have to deal with the smell of fertiliser. The same goes for shoppers of a feed supply store. Certain odours are understandable and may even appeal to the customer's sense of smell. However, shoppers don't want to smell an employee's lunch drifting across the store. Use neutralizers to combat any offensive odours.

8. **Crowded Aisles**

   Consumers like a selection but not if it means sacrificing comfort while shopping. Be sure your store is designed to allow adequate space between aisles and keep walkways free of merchandise. Cramped spaces can ruin a shopping experience and turn off a customer.

9. **Disorganised checkout counters**

   A stack of hangers, returned merchandise and sloppy work areas behind the checkout is a huge customer turn-off. This particular area where a customer's financial transaction is taking place should not show any signs of disorganisation. Like messy dressing rooms, a disorganised checkout counter can lead to theft. Keep those register areas neat and tidy.

10. **Lack of shopping carts/baskets**

    Your type of retail shop may not require a shopping cart or your store may be too small, but there's not a single type of retailer that wouldn't need at least some sort of shopping basket. If you hope for your customer to purchase more than one item in your store, be sure to have an adequate supply of shopping carts or baskets on hand.

❑❑❑

10
Methods To Protect Your Business

Thorough preparation is important when planning your business. Part of your business plan should include limiting your personal legal exposure as well as that of your business. Involving a lawyer during the planning stage could save you hassles and money later on. The following is a run down on some of the legal issues you can plan for before you start your business.

Business Structure

Choosing whether or not to incorporate or form a limited liability company for your business is one of the most important business decisions you need to make. If your business is not in one of these two structures, you will be subject to personal liability for the debts of your business. This means that your personal losses could exceed your investment in the business. With a corporation or limited liability company, your losses are limited to the amount of your investment in the business. If your business is one that involves potential liability, you should strongly consider forming either a corporation or limited liability company.

If you decide you don't need the protection of a corporation or limited liability company, and instead will operate your business as a partnership with others, you will need a written partnership agreement. This will cover the rights and responsibilities of all of the parties, as well as addressing in advance several "what if" scenarios.

Intellectual Property

Do you expect your business to be successful because you have some new product that no one else does? Or do you have a better way of doing things than your competitors? - Do you have some special knowledge that makes you better than the competition? If you have any of these things going for your business, you need to protect them or you may find that your competitors are using your competitive edge. Get a patent to protect any inventions or new processes that your business will use. You may want to trademark the unique name of your business or products as well. As for that special know how, that is considered a trade secret. You'll want to implement plans to protect any trade secrets as well.

Employment Agreements and Other Contracts

If you will be hiring employees, you should think carefully about the terms of their employment. Will they be at-will employees, who can quit or be fired at anytime? Or do you want an employment contract to make sure that a key person works for you for at least a minimum period of time? You also need to think about confidentiality agreements and non-compete agreements with your employees to keep them from telling the competition your business secrets or going to work for a competitor. You will also want to think about confidentiality and non-disclosure agreements with other people your business comes into contact with. You don't want the person you're trying to bring on as an investor to take your business idea for his own. As for other contracts, think about how big of an impact the contract will have on your business. The bigger the impact of the contract, the more important it becomes to have your lawyer participate in its negotiation.

These are just a few of the legal issues you should address before you start doing business. A lawyer who practices in the area of business law can help you with these and many others.

How do Protect a Good Business Idea from Competitors?

Ensuring that the creative thinkers in this economy are financially rewarded and their ideas are protected from pirating is an important step in ensuring that new ideas will continue to flow and stimulate our economy. For this reason, laws have been devised that protect what is called intellectual property. Intellectual property is any form of creativity. It includes inventions, discoveries, original data, unique materials, artistic works, or anything creative considered having value.

Intellectual property protection falls into four areas:

- Copyrights
- Patents
- Trademarks
- Trade secrets

A copyright gives its author exclusive rights to reproduce certain types of work for a specified period of time. Copyrights protect literary, dramatic, musical, and artistic works. Computer software is also covered by copyright laws. Copyright protection does have its limitations. Copyrights prohibit the reproduction of materials but not the ideas communicated. Also, in some cases, limited excerpts from copyrighted materials can be reproduced with appropriate acknowledgement without securing the permission of the author or copyright holder.

Patents are an exclusive right to produce, use, and sell an invention or process. The process for patenting a product can be very involved and time consuming and will generally require the assistance of a lawyer or other professional. Patentable innovations must first prove a degree of technical sophistication and uniqueness. It is surprising how often the same truly unique invention has been conceived by different individuals. That is why a patent search is an important and tedious part of the process. It is the inventor's responsibility to prove that no one else "owns" that innovation. In some cases, a concept for an invention or process is already so widely disseminated that it is considered public domain and consequently is no one's to own.

Trademarks are symbols, logos, designs, words, or letters used by a manufacturer or other business to distinguish its product or service from that of its competitors. In short, a trademark is a brand name. Even audio clips can be trademarked. A small trademark symbol, an "R" inside a circle (®), can be found on most commercially marketed products.

Trade secrets are defined as any design, process, composition, device, technique, or any unique thing that only you, or a limited group of people, are aware of and that is commercially valuable. Trade secrets tend to be limited to manufacturing processes, production machines, chemical formulas, or recipes. Trade secrets are only protected by statute when the information has been gained through dishonest means such as industrial espionage or breach of confidence. Trade secrets are not protected, however, when they are discovered through examination of goods purchased in the marketplace. An example would be recreating Kentucky Fried Chicken's "secret recipe" by purchasing the chicken and experimenting with herbs until you arrive at a combination that produces a similar-tasting product.

An entrepreneur needs to be aware of the statutes concerning intellectual property not only to protect his or her own creative interests but also to avoid infringing on another person's intellectual properties. With all the new products on the market, there really are very few new ideas. Taking the necessary precautions to ensure that the ideas being used in the business are not legally owned by someone else will save valuable time, money, and legal entanglements in the future.

Secure the Future of Your Business with Basic Office Equipment

You go into business to make money. For most people, they want to be in it for the long haul. Unfortunately, we have all heard statistics about the high number of businesses that fold. There are some easy steps you can take to promote and protect your business today by investing in simple office equipment.

As a business owner or entrepreneur, you and your company have a legal and moral responsibility to protect your customers' personal and financial information. In addition to establishing internal policies and procedures for your employees and your business, you should consider investing in a high quality paper shredder. The Sarbanes-Oxley Act of 2002 requires these types of policies and procedures. A simple and highly effective way to ensure customer information is not compromised is to use a crosscut paper shredder. By investing in a paper shredder and establishing guidelines for its use. Paper shredders are an affordable tool, especially when you consider potential litigation costs.

As a business owner, you must make decisions about how to market your business and how you want prospective employees and clients to see your company. Whether your business has a fun and recreational purpose or a staunch and conservative direction, you will want your business communications to exude professionalism. No matter what items you sell or which services you provide, your customers want someone they can depend on and believe in to do the job right. These days, customer service horror stories are everywhere. Customers are looking for professionals in whom they can trust. Customers develop their impressions of your abilities by looking at the marketing materials you provide to them.

Since so much rests on the professionalism of your marketing materials and because you still want to keep an eye on the bottom line, you should consider purchasing a binding machine for your office. A binding machine is a surefire way to boost the image you convey when submitting proposals to potential clients. If you send proposals or other lengthy documents to prospective customers or partners, you should never send chunks of paper fastened with binder clips or, even worse, rubber bands. Bound presentations and proposals look much more professional and help to instill confidence in your firm even when you're not there to talk up the documents.

Not only are binding machines affordable, they are easy to use. With a number of varieties to choose from, you are sure to be able to find a machine that suits your budget and your business needs. You can select from three types of notebook style binding (plastic comb, wire, and coil), VeloBind (using small strips of plastic), heat-based methods with a superior look (thermal and UniBind), and others.

In addition to the message of professionalism and dependability your bound documents will communicate, bound documents also allow you to completely customize each publication. You don't have to settle for a one-sizefits-all approach when preparing customer and employee communications. You can choose to create personalized documents that symbolize the personal touch you will continue to provide after the sale.

It seems simple, but choosing the right tools for your business can save you money, protect your assets, and enhance your image. Not a bad way to start your business!

Secure the Future of Your Small Business with an Estate Plan

If you are a small-business owner, and you die, what happens? If you haven't left a similar plan of action, called an estate plan, the lives of your loved ones will be thrown into turmoil.

Without an estate plan, all sorts of problems can arise when you die:

- Your business might have to be shut down if no one knows how to run it, what to do, who your important contacts are, what accounts you have and so forth.
- Everything you own will have to be probated by the legal system. Your loved ones will have to hire attorneys, and a nice chunk of your estate will end up paying legal fees and court costs.
- Since probate is a public process, what you owned and owe will be public knowledge, and your loved ones will not see any money for up to a year, until the probate is over.
- You can avoid all of these unenviable fates if you take time now to create an estate plan for you and your small business. An estate plan is nothing more than your plan of action for how you want your assets distributed should you pass away. It utilizes various tools to effectuate your desires as quickly and inexpensively as possible.

The main parts of your estate plan include:

1. **A will or a living trust**

   Both are documents that transfer what you own to whom you want your possessions to go to when you die. But that is where the similarities end. Although a will does allow you to decide who gets what, using one still means that your assets will go through probate.

   It's better for the small-business owner to get a living trust. A living trust is similar to a corporation. It's a separate legal entity that you create and control that details what you want to have happen to your assets. Because the trust owns your assets, it leaves nothing to probate when you pass away.

   A living trust has several advantages over a will:

   - It's private.
   - It allows you to bypass probate altogether.
   - It transfers your assets immediately upon your death.
   - It saves in legal fees, court costs and estate taxes.

2. **Life insurance**

   Why are you in business for yourself? One major reason is probably to take care of your family, financially speaking. However, not all small businesses are cash cows, and many contain no value once the owner is gone. In that case, how will your family survive?

   Life insurance, especially term life insurance, is the answer. It is inexpensive, and having it means that your loved ones will have enough money to buy a home, pay for a wedding, go to college or whatever they need.

3. **IRS tax breaks**

   An estate tax (also known as the death tax) still exists. It can cost up to 50 percent of the business' value and is due nine months after you pass away. However, various IRS sections allow your beneficiaries to redeem your stock without major tax penalties or defer taxes past the nine-month deadline. Check with your CPA.

4. **Buy-sell agreements**

   If several people own your business, a buy-sell agreement is necessary. Without one, your beneficiaries may get stuck owning a business they don't want and can't sell, or your partners may get stuck with partners they didn't expect. A buy-sell agreement mandates that upon certain conditions (like the death of a shareholder or partner) parties to the agreement must sell their shares to the other parties at a fair market price.

5. **Succession plan**

   If your business is a sole proprietorship, you need a plan in place so that your heirs know how to either run things without you or sell the business. What the business owns, owes, important contacts, bank account information, and so forth must be laid out in a clear way. If you want a particular family member to run the business (or own it), you need to discuss this with that person and teach him or her, what they need to know.

How to Protect Your Good Accounts from the Competition?

Great question. This is a major threat to your business. The competition can be devastating to your business if you losing one of your good accounts. That should be enough reason for you to give special time and thought to this question.

But losing a good account impacts your business in additional negative ways. The individuals within your good accounts are typically those people who provide you special insights into what your competition is doing and what is happening in the market. Lose one of those good accounts, and you lose some of that special insight.

Your good accounts are the first places you take your new products and services. They provide you ready acceptance and honest feedback for your new offerings. You hone presentations and sharpen your approaches the feedback provided by your good accounts. Lose one of them, and that special function they provide is also gone.

And then, of course, we all knew that your good accounts are the places where you make the greatest financial return for your time invested.

So, it pays to think more deeply about how to vaccinate your good accounts from the competition's enticements. Here are four proven strategies to help you withstand competitive onslaughts.

Deepen and Broaden Your Relationships

It is difficult for your good friends to take their business away from you and give it to someone they don't know or trust as well. Not that it can't ever happen, but if you have great relationships with the key people in your good accounts, if you have turned them into friends and not just business acquaintances, you'll put a layer of protection between you and your competition. So, you need to focus on turning the contacts in your good accounts into friends by deepening and broadening your relationships.

To deepen the relationships means that you work at enabling the key people within your good accounts to know you and your company better. Take them to lunch, go to a ball game together, create an opportunity for them to meet your spouse and vice versa. Turn them into friends.

Extend the relationship to include the rest of your company. If possible, bring a number of the key people in your good accounts into your facility to meet some of your company's other employees. Take your boss, operations manager and customer service people into the account to meet them. The more comfortable they are with your company, the more of your people they know, the less likely they are to seriously consider the enticements of a motivated competitor.

To broaden the relationships means that you make sure that you know more of the key people within your key accounts, and that they know you. Be methodical. Make a list of all the important contact people within a good account. Then carefully evaluate the state of the relationship you have with each of them.

If there are important people who don't know you, fix that quickly. Make sure that you have positive relationships with your key contact's boss, and the boss's boss. Work as high up the hierarchy as possible.

While the depth and breath of your relationship isn't a foolproof vaccination against your competitors, it goes a long way to assuring that your good account will keep you informed of what is happening, and will probably give you an opportunity to respond to any especially appealing enticements. It's step one in protecting yourself from the competition.

Close Any Open Doors

Your competitors will be looking for ways to gain a foothold in your accounts. They'll search for cracks in the door that they can wedge into greater opportunities. Beat them to the punch by eliminating any opportunities. Carefully examine these issues:

1. **Pricing**

   It is not at all unusual to find that some prices in your good accounts have crept up to the point where they are not nearly as competitive as they may be in other places.

Review your prices, and make sure that your margin increases haven't put you in an awkward position. You may have to reduce some prices to prevent a competitor from making you look bad.

2. **Problems**

There may be some unresolved, lingering problems in your account. And, while they may not seem important to you, they provide an opportunity for your competitors to turn into an opportunity for them.

Are there products that need to be returned? Invoices with discrepancies that need to be resolved? Items that need to be picked up? Training that was to have been done and never got scheduled? Information you were supposed to obtain for someone that you never did?

You've got the idea. If there are any unresolved problems in the account, a good competitor will find them and exploit them to his advantage and your disadvantage.

3. **Products**

You may have some product weaknesses that you competitor can exploit. For example, you may have available this year's version of some standard product. But your good customer is happy using an earlier version. You've never seen any reason to try to convert them to this year's model, when they are perfectly happy with last year's. However, last year's model may not stand up favourably to this year's version for your competition. In that case, you may look bad when your competitor brings in this year's hot new product, and compares it to an older model that you are supplying. Shame on you. You should have detailed your version before your competitor got the chance.

Bundle up Your Products and Services

You may be selling ten different items to one of your good accounts. Rather than continue to sell those ten as separate issues, package them together and write a contract that addresses all of them as a package deal. Get your good customer to acknowledge the package. That way, if your competitor tries to pick out one of the items you're selling, they can't because the price and service on one item impacts the others. The more you can bundle items together into packages the more difficult it is for your competition to dislodge you on one of those items.

Formally Communicate Your Value

Arrange for quarterly meetings between your good customer's key people and you and your boss. At these meetings, bring reports detailing aspects of your service, how much money you've saved that customer, the training you've done, the information you've provided, etc. Don't be afraid to identify other areas that you could impact in the same way. This formal reporting raises your position in the customer's eyes from that of being just a vendor, to that of a valuable partner. This separates you from the competition, and makes it less likely that your customer will be attracted to the someone else.

While none of these strategies are guaranteed to put an impenetrable wall around your good accounts, the wise combination of them will make penetrating one of your good accounts an extremely difficult and frustrating project for your competitors. Sometimes the best strategy is a good defense.

❑❑❑